CRUEL LEGACY

**An introduction to the
record of Deaf People
in History**

by

A F Dimmock

Published by Scottish Workshop Publications

      Donaldson's College

      West Coates

      Edinburgh

      EH12 5JJ

      Scotland

British Library Cataloguing in Publication Data
ISBN 1 873577 30 3

Typeset & Laserprinted by   Susan Napier & Gordon Davidson,

                                   Donaldson's College

Cover by Colin White

To Jean with Love

CHAPTER	CONTENTS	PAGE NO

Foreword

It was only during the past decade recognition of the importance in preserving Deaf history has emerged. In the main, Deaf heritage, culture and folklore has been passed down from generation to generation via the medium of sign language and fingerspelling. Due to this new found pastime there has been an upsurge of deaf and hearing writers in the field of Deaf history, which is welcome by the majority who take pride in preserving history and also by members of British Deaf community anxious to discover their heritage and the roots pertaining to Deaf culture and history. It is also vital that the history of Deaf people is made available to future generations, especially Deaf schoolchildren as part of their history lessons.

In his book, "Cruel Legacy", Arthur Frederick Dimmock, better known as 'Dimmock' has drawn upon experience gained from more than half a century travelling the five continents of the globe as a tour director and researcher into Deaf history. Wherever Dimmock travelled, he always made a point of checking the local history for reference to Deaf issues and happenings to Deaf people. This news enabled him to amass a personal collection of historical facts pertaining to deafness and Deaf history. Much of the content of this book has not been available in this country before.

In his book, "Cruel Legacy", Dimmock leads the reader to ancient Greek/Biblical writings, which tell us there was sign language in use by the Deaf as far back as 422 BC. The book continues with the amazing story of Deaf history throughout past centuries revealing noble accomplishments by Deaf artists and professionals also covering various deeds by hearing people to make the Deaf communicate by sign language and by attempts to make them talk.

Writings have been published and papers given about the infamous 'Milan Resolution' in 1880. However, in this book, credit is due to Dimmock for giving

I

the most detailed insight to the reasons and actions of the main characters of that era, before and after the resolution. This fascinating account also described how countries in Europe and elsewhere persuaded to adopt the resolution banning sign language in Deaf education, despite protests from the already fluently educated Deaf community, who had studied via sign language, and as Dimmock rightly states, were not consulted.

After reading this book, the reader should have not the slightest doubt that Deaf people have a rich and cultural heritage and despite the 'Milan hiccup' should be in full control of their lives and their destiny. "Cruel Legacy" should become a history text book in all schools for the Deaf and go hand in hand with teaching Deaf studies by both Deaf and hearing where Deaf children will learn of the great men and women who are part of their heritage, as was so clearly recommended by George Montgomery, way back in 1978, when he named the great Deaf stalwarts, Beethoven, Goya, Keller, Lacroix and Wellington. I am sure if Dr Montgomery wrote that today he would have added the writer Dimmock who has given us a fine contribution to the Deaf legacy he writes about.

A Murray Holmes
Chairman - British Deaf Association

Introduction

The birth of an idea emancipated when Deaf communities from all over the world gathered at Brussels during the Summer, 1953, to participate in the 7th International Games of the Deaf. The instigator of the idea was Frere Majorin, a monk attached to the teaching staff at the Woluwe-Saint-Lambert School for the Deaf and Blind just outside the city. He was a scholar, writer, linguist and an editor of a monthly that dealt with affairs of the Deaf. Prior to the Games, he sent out invitations to editors and writers to come to an exhibition of magazines and writings of the Deaf World. At that time I was the editor of Independent Courier and a club magazine, The Review, so I received an invitation. During the week-long exhibition I met a number of writers and reporters and exchanged addresses with them. This led to a widespread connection that lasted to this day. Up to the time of the exhibition I was in touch with a small number of editors and writers in France who supplied me with topics of their world. As contacts increased I became a large receiver, probably the largest ever, of Deaf news and stories. The most striking, especially the ones touching repression and suppression of Deaf people, were stored and given vent in this book.

All the material duly gathered and mentioned in British Deaf Times and later in British Deaf News, and other relevant publications amount to a vast collection and would make this book unwieldy and reading it would be a humdrum. The book's purpose is to reveal how badly Deaf people were treated in the course of history. There are some characters in the book who appear to have been spared the ordeals of many such as Juan Fernandez Navarette, known as The Mute, whose charmed life begot envious enemies but he was protected by being the King's favourite. Another such person was Emmanuel Philbert, the Deaf Mute Ambassador, who had a highly elated life but he was mocked by so many behind his back through being unable to hear.

Not all the material came from writings. Some were gathered during my travels resulting in meeting people unable to express themselves in words. Deaf people, like myself, using signing as a first language are naturally endowed with a form of gesticulation that can be used in Deaf communities all over the world and understood with remarkable clarity. I have had discourses, some very long, with Bantu people in South Africa, the Moorish in North Africa, the Aborigines in Australia, the Moujiks in Russia, the Greek Islands peasantry and the Spanish gypsies. Among the latter, I met a woman who lived on rats during the aftermath of the Spanish Civil War and this diet, she said, made her sparklingly healthy. Some were in distressing conditions and had to soldier on. Almost all said they were treated like dirt and were not helped along by the authorities and had to rely heavily on their families for succour in the form of shelter, food, clothing and a little money.

A F Dimmock
June, 1993

The Legacy of Antiquity

Chapter One

Rising at dawn one notices a ragged and haggard group, scavaging the streets for food or chattels. An immediate cry from the throat of the early riser rents the air and in response, people come running to the scene. They know what the alarm was about so they come armed with sticks, staves and stones. The ashen faced horde, too weak to resist the blows and prods, flee, as best as they are able to their isolated place in the desert, well away from the habitation of the people. The victims are lepers.

Persecution of the diseased, disabled, deviationist and ethnic minorities fill the course of history. Woe betide the peculiar in small numbers for they are trampled underfoot by the conventional many. The Deaf, particularly those with unintelligible speech, have been shunned, mocked and forced into a rigid normalisation process which often fails.

One of the earliest known references to the Deaf came from the mouth of Aristotle (384-322 BC). He implied that the Deaf could not possibly be taught to speak. Their tongues were tied and, therefore, to teach them to speak would be to court ridicule. This was a tremendous and lasting disservice to the deaf because no educated person would waste his time and strength in essaying an acknowledged impossibility. The doctrines of Aristotle became common knowledge over the civilised world and made a lasting impact for almost 2,000 years. In the ancient and medieval worlds it was obvious that speech was believed to be an instinct, not an acquired art, on which hearing had no influence and the exercise was automatically impossible for the Deaf. The tongue-tied theory inhibited the working of an innate gift. Authorities treated Aristotle with respect and handed down his theory in garbled form from generation to generation. Even the Christian Church fully endorsed it because their outlook was essentially teleological which implied that

1

speech is an instinct rendered null and impossible by deafness. St Augustine (354-430 AD) came under the influence of the Aristotle theory and said "For what great fault innocence is sometimes born blind and sometimes born deaf which blemish indeed hinders faith as witness the apostle who says that faith comes by hearing." Augustine and later church leaders held standfastly to the theory that faith cannot be given except through hearing and in this case the Deaf cannot know God. They endorsed Aristotle. The Deaf were, therefore, beyond human help unless there was a divine intervention following the Biblical stories relating to Christ's cure of the deaf and dumbman.

Earlier in 422 BC Socrates on the other hand noticed the existence of the earliest form of sign language. He commented "If we have no voice or tongue and wished to make things clear to one another should we not try, as the dumb actually do, to make signs with our hands, head and person generally?" This was an acknowledgement that the Deaf, although voiceless, can communicate in a more or less intelligent form. His thoughts were not, unfortunately, given serious consideration by other philosophers of the time, particularly Aristotle.

The earliest Western mention of a deaf man is found in the book of Herodotus, the Greek historian, and also with some differences in the "Cyropaedia" of Xenophon. The instance is the deaf son of Croesus, King of Lydia. King Croesus lived from about 550 to 600 BC, which was more than a hundred years before Herodotus wrote. There was ample scope for myths and legends which the author was fond of incorporating in his History. With the growth of Greek and Lydian folklore the true personality of the deaf prince became hopelessly entangled with legend. But in some allusions to him we get glimpses of the state of mind of the ancients towards the Deaf. Croesus had two sons, of whom one was grievously afflicted, for he was dumb; but the other, Atys, far surpassed all the men of his age. In Greek the word, Kophos, meant deaf as well as dumb. Speaking to his son Atys, the King is represented as saying "You are my only son; the other, who is deprived of hearing, I consider as lost. Atys became famous as the subject of one of the numerous legends centred about King Croesus and his name had to be preserved in tradition to distinguish him from the other "the deaf son" who outlived Atys and finally found favour with his father. Atys was accidentally killed in a boar hunt. Concerning the deaf son, Croesus consulted the mysterious Voice at the Temple of Apollo at Delphi and the answer given to him was "O Lydian-born, King of many people, foolish Croesus, do not crave to hear the voice of thy son speaking within thy palace; it is better for thee that this event should be far off, for he will first speak on an unhappy day." On another occasion the oracle, which was supposed to see all and know all, had identified the King beyond doubt by saying to him "I understand the dumb, and hear him that does not speak." This may be an indication that it was known that Croesus knew how to converse with his deaf son by some code of signs.

Croesus' kingdom became prosperous and powerful but the King was superstitious and the oracle was his undoing. Apollo's voice from the depth of the Delphian temple told him that if he made war on the Persians he would overthrow a great empire. Herodotus brings the deaf son into the story when Croesus' army is defeated and his cities taken. A Persian soldier rushed on Croesus to kill him but this speechless son of his, when he saw the Persian advancing burst into speech begging the man not to kill his father. These were the first words he ever uttered and after this he was speaking for the remainder of his life. In the legend he saved his father's life but the kingdom was lost and the one and only deaf man who might have been King never emerged.

The period between the 5th and 6th century BC saw Sparta as Greece's military might. A sinister discipline was in force to achieve it. This meant subjecting male children and youth to the vigours of physical exercise and fighting practice, leading to the eventual goal as valiant warriors. The females were also engaged in such body training activities so that when time came they might bear stalwart sons. The Spartans are the only people in history who dared to carry out the principles of modern eugenics which Hitler was later to copy. At birth, a baby was taken away from its parents for the elders of the tribe to examine. It is was plump and strong, they said "Rear it." If not, it was exposed to die in the cleft of a mountain, for they

3

thought it was better for it and the city. A remarkable few were known to survive and return whereupon they were made welcome for being so strong and to keep alive against all odds. For the crippled, blind and deaf the fate was far worse. They were taken to Taygete Cliff and hurled right into the waters of Barathre and certain death. The Deaf, usually discovered during or soon after infancy, even though physically perfect and sturdy, were thought to be impossible to instruct under the Spartan code that demands absolute obedience to all its teaching and commands. Failure to obey meant dreadful punishment, sometimes resulting in death. Parents separated from their offspring at the onset knew nothing of its fate so they were spared the anguish. The prescribed order for such a harsh and fateful life was the result of the Lycurgus Laws formed about the 9th century BC after a lawgiver of that name.

In contrast, Persia, Greece's long standing enemy, and Egypt regarded the Deaf as privileged in heaven and favoured by the gods. They were thought to be gifted with wisdom but prevented by divine intervention from disclosing any of it. They were venerated and given certain rights that enabled them to live in harmony without sinking into poverty or slavery which was the usual perception for the deaf elsewhere.

530 AD is believed to be the year that hearing people first thought about deaf people's rights. Roman authors of Justinian Code included the needs of deaf people in the law. The Code identified five classifications or combinations of deafness and muteness. It was in one respect unfavourable to the born deaf. They were classified as idiots and aliens and their disability was equalled to death. However, even with this law, it never occurred to the ancient Romans and Greeks that a person born deaf could be educated. Only one such person, QuintusPedius, is mentioned in all the surviving Roman literature. He was the son of a consul of the same name and co-heir of Augustus. Although deaf and dumb, his talents as a painter and artist won the approval of the divine Augustus. The historian, Pliny, left an elaborate record of him.

Quintus Pedius

At the time, the Roman Empire was under threat and after its collapse all was forgotten andat the advent of Christianity, the Augustine theory dominated people's thoughts towards the deaf. The dumb boy of Hexham, England, who was taught to speak by St John of Beverley,Bishop of Hagulstad, in the 7th century failed to attract sufficient interest among church dignitaries to commend the theory. The historian, Bede, wrote that this occurred in 685 AD and represented the process of teaching the boy as a single instantaneous action or miracle. This mention of miracle was rather unfortunate as it tended to play into the hands of Augustine theorists.

The deaf and dumb were regarded as a class apart and this made them victims of working out of gregarious instinct. Like sparrows attacking a canary, hearing people have for centuries vented their spite against circumstance of these hapless creatures. Such animal cruelty went on ceaselessly till the beginning of the 19th century in most advanced countries but elsewhere it continued unabated. In a civilised country like Italy as recently as 1975 police Inspector Delle Corte heard rumours that led him to the Adriatic Village of Arti to interview one Fiorangelo Ferratti, and to ask him about his brother, Carmine. The inspector was led to a pigsty and in a dark corner he saw something stirring. It was Carmine. He was kept there for 60 years, firstly by his parents, then by his brother and finally the sons of the brother. He never saw lights and lived on pig food. He contracted meningitis when he was 7 and became deaf and dumb as a result. His parents thought it was an act of God punishing him for some misdeed. To them it was a great shame so they shut him off from the world. Fiorangelo and his sons received prison sentences. Carmine was taken to hospital but died before recovery. Such an attitude towards the deaf was not unusual among the peasantry and still exists to this day in some undeveloped countries.

It was probably not generally known that the daughter of one of the English Kings was deaf and dumb. Katherine Plantagenet, the youngest child of Henry III was born on St Katherine's Day, November 25th, 1253. Her christening feast was celebrated with great pomp and rejoicing. Some items of the bill of fare consisted of 14 wild boars, 24 swans, 250 partridges, 1,650 fowls, 61,000 eggs, etc. The little princess was styled as the queen's beautiful daughter and was described as a remarkably lovely child.

It was not till she was about 2 years old when her royal parents realised the sad fact that their daughter was deaf and dumb. The distressed King made large offerings to Westminster Abbey on numerous occasions on Katherine's behalf. The prayers of the sorrowing parents were surely answered, though not as they themselves had hoped, as the lovely little deaf mute was not left to grow up in ignorance and helplessness which was the fate of all thus afflicted in these days. In 1257, the ears which had been deaf to all mortal sounds heard the voice of angels calling her to Paradise at the early age of 32.

Katherine's health had always been delicate and the year before she died she had been sent for some time to the country to be under the charge of the widowed Lady

Emma de St John, tenant of one of the Crown Manors in Berkshire known at the time as Swalefelle, later as the Village of Swallowfield. The King sent, among other presents, a little kid from the Royal Forests to be her playfellow at Swallowfield. He continually despatched messengers to enquire about her health and once, when the report was better than usual, he bestowed in his delight a good robe to the messenger who brought the welcome tidings. But the child was fast fading away from the earth and she only returned to Windsor to die on 3rd May, 1257. The King and Queen were inconsolable in their daughter's loss and Henry fretted himself into a low fever. Costly gifts were bestowed upon her nurses in remembrance of the sweet little maiden. A gorgeous funeral was held at Westminster Abbey and a silver statue as large as life was placed over her tomb as the last proofs of love by her heart-broken parents. The statue was stolen during the dissolution and all that remains is a tomb devoid of any inscription of the deceased.

Who knows that she, being a princess, might have had an instructor provided for her had she lived longer and might have supplied a chapter in history of education of the deaf. Even in the rude era, England had its learned and compassionate priests such as St John of Beverley 4 centuries before Princess Katherine's time and the opportunity would not have been lacking in the royal court or in the silences of Swallowfield for experiment in teaching the deaf and thus giving them a place of respect in society.

Social and legal matters treated the deaf and dumb as pariahs and insurmountable handicaps were set against them when applying for welfare and legal redress. In Spain during the 14th and 15th centuries some noble men had heirs who were deaf and dumb. In the eyes of the law they could not inherit a title and it was argued that because of their being dumb they could not be responsible for discharging the numerous duties which office holders are subject to.

The Spanish Contribution

Chapter Two

In 1526, Juan Fernandez Navarette was born of noble parents at Logrono in Spain. He was destined to change the scene of common thought towards the Deaf. He lost his hearing at the age of 3 and had no speech. At the time, there were no teachers of the deaf, so he grew up uneducated. It was his fondness of drawing that brought him attention that resulted in something approaching an education. In early childhood he took to expressing his wants and ideas by rough sketches in chalk or charcoal, and showed much skill in the medium of expression as other children of his age do in speaking. His father placed him in the care of artist-monk, Friar Vincent de Santo Domingo who dwelt in the Monastery of the Star, near Logrono. The friar taught him all he knew about drawing and painting and there were some who thought that the teaching of the three R's would have interfered with the making of a great artist. The only equivalent of college the friar could visualise for his deaf pupil was travel and when Navarrete reached young manhood he went to Florence, Rome, Naples and Milan. When he saw the paintings of the great masters and learned to appreciate their excellence, the result was a desire to imitate only the best. Titian greatly influenced him. When he returned to Spain he was sufficiently reputed as an artist to interest Don Luis. Manrique, who was Grand Almoner or dispenser of favours at the court of Philip II, King of Spain, invited him to Madrid and secured him an appointment as painter to the King. At the court he was known as El Mudo (the mute). He was also nicknamed the "Spanish Titian". All his paintings were on religious subjects, the most popular theme in Spain during the 16th century. His most famous is "Abraham Receiving the Three Angels". Some faces in his paintings were drawn from life. Having taken a dislike of Santoys, the Royal Secretary, the deaf artist consigned him to eternal obliquity by painting his face on the shoulders of one of the wicked men who tortured St James the Apostle. Santoys complained to the King but the monarch considered it a great joke and stood by the painter and refused to order any alterations. Here was, indeed, an instance of genius not waiting for education and giving cause for questioning the advantages of formal education over self-developed talents. One historian said of him "He read and wrote and played at cards, and expressed his meaning by signs with singular clearness."

From other accounts it seems, however, that signs were his chief reliance in conversation. He died on 28th March, 1579, at Toledo leaving a series of uncompleted pictures. The Spanish poet, Lope de Vega, composed his epitaph with the words "Heaven denied me speech, that by my understanding I might greater feeling give to the things which I painted: and such great life did I give them with my skilful pencil, that, as I could not speak, I made them speak for me." Lope wrote furthermore: "This artist painted no face that was dumb" which is not to be interpreted on any supposition that dumb people look any different from others, but merely that the faces which Navarrete drew expressed eloquently the thoughts that were behind them.

It was probably Juan Fernandez Navarrete who jolted the nobles who had deaf children into thought and action. Just as the painter's father sought a monk to teach his son art, they found another to educate their children and to make them speak, a faculty which in their view was the imperative aim. The monk chosen, Pedro Ponce de Leon, resided in the nearby monastery of Ona. There were instances of earlier educated deaf mutes but the first systematic education began in Spain, some time before 1550. Ponce had several pupils who were deaf and dumb from birth, sons of great lords and notable people. He taught them to speak, read, write, pray, to assist at Mass and to know the doctrines of Christianity. The most noted of these pupils, and the only ones recorded in Spanish history, were the brothers Don Francisco and Don Pedro, of the house of Tobar, a branch of the eminent de Velasco family who were influential subjects of the King of Castile. The deaf brethren were the sons of Juan de Velasco, Marquis of Berlanga. Don Francisco was, by priority of age, heir to the Marquisate and certain legal questions came up on account of his deafness. It could be argued that, as the deaf and dumb were excluded from responsibility under the law of the Middle Ages, they could not inherit a title. A learned lawyer, the licentiate Lasso, was invited to the Monastery of Ona to witness with his own eyes the great novelty of the deaf and dumb being taught to speak, read and write. He remained long enough to write to Don Francisco a lengthy and florid Treatise, which has been preserved, and which presented the marvellous results of Ponce's teaching and proved from 8 different points of view - with much legal subtlety - that on account of having recovered his speech, Don Francisco could claim his right to the Marquisate, having abrogated the law by removing the 'casus' and intent of the law which was based on his "dumbness". An interesting portion of the argument is that where Lasso seeks to prove that few men possess perfect speech - probably intended to guard against any mistakes in Don Francisco's speech, should a legal test be made of his ability to speak.

It was not known if the matter came up in the courts but Don Francisco's fortunes were good for in 1578 Ponce de Leon wrote on the subject of his pupils, mentioning no names, that one of them had succeeded to an estate and marquisate, entered the army and proved to be skilled in the use of arms and was especially a good rider. His other attainments were the knowledge of Spanish, Latin, natural philosophy and history. He died young without apparently leaving any descendants. His brother, Don Pedro, became noted in another manner. According to the King's historiographer, Ambrosio de Morales, he mastered Latin and Greek in addition to Spanish. Although totally deaf, he was reputed to have led the monks in the monastery in chanting, keeping time and tune so that the music was in perfect order. In a legal document dated 24th August, 1578, instituting the foundation of a chapel, there appears to be some evidence that Don Pedro de Tobar was ordained and held office and emolument in the church and performed the service of the Canonic Hours. A career in the Church would naturally fall to the lot of a younger son of the Marquis of Berlanga, who would inherit no title. Benefices in the Church were in those days conferred on men with strong family support. Don Pedro's hearing brother was Count of Haro and Constable of Castile, hereditary offices which brought great power with them. It is appropriate to say that only by the aid of connections such as these that a candidate, deaf or hearing, could obtain exalted church offices in the 16th century. Don Pedro had two deaf sisters who entered a nunnery and spent the rest of their lives there.

Ponce de Leon died about 1585 and left no writings on how he taught the deaf but before his demise one Juan Pablo Bonet contacted him and learnt something about teaching the deaf. Bonet was employed in some secretarial capacity by the Duke and Duchess of Frias, who had a born deaf son, Don Luis. He noted the Duchess' efforts to find a cure for her son's deafness, making all enquiries of different persons, and sparing no expense that the noble gentleman might not be left unaided and this involved in her secretary seeking out Ponce. Bonet's actions were quick and the result gave him universal acclaim as the inventor of dactylogy, better known as the manual alphabet, which was later to influence the French innovator, Michel, Abbé de l'Epée, despite the much earlier written description of a manual alphabet by St Bede which is usually overlooked. Following Ponce's footsteps, Bonet took Don Luis de Velasco as his first pupil. Born about 1604, he was the great-nephew of Don Francisco de Tobar and younger brother of Bernardino Hernandez de Valesco, the Constable of Castile, who was a constant attendant and influential figure at the court of King Philip IV of Castile. Don Luis must have been the first named person in history to use the one-handed alphabet and in addition his teacher taught him to speak and lipread exceptionally well. In 1628, King Philip IV of Castile made him the first Marquis of Fresno, most likely in recognition of his educational attainment and speaking ability. This title made him one better than his deaf great-uncle and it was not through inheritance but by creation. Five years earlier his brother, the Constable, introduced him to the Prince of Wales, later Charles I, during the Prince's visit to Madrid. The Prince spoke words in English which the deaf man reproduced correctly. He called it "One of the wonders of Spain". Bonet wrote a book about his achievements, taking care to leave out any mention of Ponce thus allowing the impression to get about that the method was entirely original with himself. Don Luis de Velasco died in 1664.

At the same time there came along another teacher of the deaf in the person of Manuel Ramirez de Carrion who had already experienced teaching a young deaf nobleman, Alfonso Fernandez de Cordova y Gigueroa, Marquis of Priego. He also instructed Don Juan Alonso de Medina, of the noble house of Medina-Celi. There were several other noble pupils whom he taught to speak in a way everybody understood. In later years he rose to new eminence as the tutor of the deaf Prince of Carignan, son of the ruler of Savoy. Carrion also wrote a book about his work "Marvels of Nature" in turn he left out any mention of Ponce and Bonet.

The deaf of the nobility and the rich were given all that needed to be taught, respect, legal recognition and accession. These of the commoners, particularly the peasantry, continued to be treated like outcasts. Not to know God or to deny the godhead's existence was the greatest disgrace in Spain at that time.

There is, however, a theory that among the Benedictine and Order of St Jerome monks, who were subjected to vows of silence, developed a cognitive form of signed communication thus providing a way to circumvent their vows of silence. This well-developed home sign became their norm and this must have lead to their reasoning that lack of speech was not symptomatic to lack of reasoning. Nevertheless, the general thought that existed for centuries was that anyone, particularly the Deaf, without speech were uneducatable. Apparently these monks provided the key that led to the education of the Deaf. That must have been how Friar Vincent, Ponce, Bonet and others responded. Ponce undertook the instruction of the Deaf in ideal circumstances that is in the heart of long established signing community and in the same circumstances other monks in another signing order could have quite conceivably been moved to do the same. Some argue that this was the very beginning of education of the Deaf even though Ponce was requested to enable his noble pupils to speak so that they could inherit their hereditary title and legal rights. It appears, unarguably, that he started teaching them by sign till they became sufficiently proficient in written language before paving their way to speech.

Anyone without language or education, having artistic propensities of a higher order, has been subject to hypothesis. Such was the case of Hendrik Avercamp, (1585 - 1634). There was no evidence that he was schooled although his father was a schoolmaster who later became an apothecary and his grandfather was Petrus Meerhoutanus, a famous sage at the time. To ,conceal his deaf mutism, which was associated with idiocy, his family most obviously described him as extremely taciturn but the locals called him "den stomme van Kempen" (the mute of Kempen). He lived at Kempen most of his life but was taught painting by Pieter Isaacsz at Amsterdam and influenced by Gillis van Coninxloo and particularly by Pieter Brueghel, the elder. On her death bed his mother bequeathed her money to her "deaf and pitiable son so that he shall not burden his brothers and sisters." Little did she know that the paintings of the born deaf artist subsequently became the finest masterpieces of winter scenes that reached astronomical values. He found inspiration for his work in the social life of the townsfolks, enjoying their winter amusements and merry carnivals on ice, and in the countryside along the Ijsel river. Avercamp was believed to have been commissioned by Frederick V Elector Palatine and King of Bohemia, who was forced to seek refuge in Holland in 1620, to do a painting of himself driving a sleigh in which was seated a masked figure believed to be Elizabeth, daughter of Charles I, of England. The painting done in 1621 is now in the Ryler Museum Haarlem. Attempts to conceal Avercamp's disability have been made by historians in Holland because of the stigma but elsewhere it came to light. The present day association of Deaf Artists in the Netherlands is proudly named after him.

A deaf man holds a place in European history, as one of the potent Princes who managed to retain their possessions in the turbulent 17th century, when Louis XIV of France was keeping every other neighbouring nation in arms fighting either for him or against him. This man of Italian descent was named Emmanuele Filberto Amedee Carignano and he held court at Turin, a key city in the path of any army invading Italy from France and vice-versa. His territory as Prince of the House of Savoy consisted of all the land around the village of Carignano, some 11 miles south of Turin and he was nephew and cousin of successive Dukes of Savoy who held the balance of power between the armies of France and Spain. He was also related by descent to the royal families of both contending countries. Francis I of France and Philip II of Spain were among the names of his great-grandparents. In later years he was known widely as the uncle of Prince Eugene of Savoy who reaped fame as a military genius.

Known by his French name, Emmanuel Philbert was born deaf at Moutiers, Switzerland, on 20th August 1628. His father Thomas de Savoia commanded the Spanish armies from 1635 - 1640. It was probably while sojourning in Spain he heard of the celebrated teacher of the Deaf, Manuel Ramirez de Carrion, and he promptly engaged him to tutor his son, who possessed in infancy "all the spirit, sense and intelligence" of the House of Savoy although unable to hear or speak. Other tutors thus engaged were Vincenzio Darini, an Italian and Claude Vaugelas, a French educator.

Several efforts were made to enable the boy to hear and speak. Carrion came up with the promise to make him do so but on the condition that his parents would leave him completely in the instructor's charge for several years and not interfere with him or even inquire as to what he was doing. The truth is that Carrion used him as dog-trainers do, and those men at times exhibit for money all sorts of animals whose tricks and obedience astonish everybody, seeming to understand and to express by signs all that their master tells them, coerced by hunger, the whip, confinement in the dark and rewards in proportion. All authorities tend to agree that the course of study Emmanuel Philbert underwent was a severe one and he was all the better off for it. He was able to speak although not perfectly and read lips quite well. A historian of the time, Louis de Rouvroy, Duke of Saint-Simon, who wrote forty volumes of gossipy memoirs mentioned him as "this famous mute, so wise and capable". He had a knowledge of several languages and sciences.

A quote made by Emmanuel Philbert appears in the writing of another historian, Tallement des Reaux, which states that he would not ever wish to marry, on account of the fact that any woman would scorn to have him. It is believed that he was referring to his deafness as the obstacle to marriage but the years were to diminish his apprehension towards matrimony, and in 1664 he was united to Angelica Catherine d'Este, a noblewoman of the House of Modena. The marriage was conducted in secret and believed to have been encouraged by the present Duke of Savoy, Philbert's cousin, for political reasons. When the news finally reached the court of King Louis XIV a year later there was a small tempest. The King had notions of his own about making a match for Philbert, and had a connection in his mind for him. The lady in question was Mademoiselle d'Angouleme - quoted in the memoirs of the King's cousin, Anna Marie, Duchess of Montpensier as "the union of a deaf-mute to a fool".

Emmanuel Philbert's father, Thomas, Prince of Carignano, died in 1656 and the deaf son succeeded him as the second Prince of the dynasty. In the preceding year Prince Thomas had joined France against Italy and led 20,000 Frenchmen in the Siege of Pavia. In this siege, Emmanuel Philbert took part and acquitted himself bravely enough to obtain mention in the biographical dictionaries as a soldier. The Duke of Savoy had a high appreciation of the deaf Prince's ability and when he thought he was going to die of small-pox, he named him as the one worth to inherit his ducal crowns. But the Duke recovered and the title was passed to a son, born later.

In 1701 occurred an event which had mistakenly added an Ambassadorship to the accomplishments of this remarkable deaf man. Ripley, of the "Believe it or Not" fame mentioned him as "Deaf-Mute Ambassador" which was founded on a misunderstanding of Saint-Simon's account of the betrothal of King Philip V of Spain. Ripley's statement refers to Emmanuel Philbert as the Spanish King's appointed Ambassador to Savoia. Actually the deaf Prince was not sent from Spain to Savoy but was right there on his own home ground. The real Ambassador Extraordinary, sent by Philip was Charles Homodei Pachaceo, Marquis d'Alondacid y de Castel-Rodrigo. He brought a proposal from King Philip to marry Princess Maria Louisa of Savoy, a cousin of Emmanuel Philbert. The deaf man's part in the transaction was simply as proxy for the absent King Philip in formally presenting this proposal to the lady. The procuration or authorisation of proxy was originally intended for the Duke of Savoy but he passed it on to Emmanuel Philbert perhaps moved by political caution, but ostensibly out of regard to the latter's worthiness.

In 1706 Emmanuel Philbert and his whole family were captured by the French and taken from Turin to an isolated locality, where they left under parole in their own concentration camp, until the war ended. He died on 23rd April, 1709, and the court of Louis XIV went into mourning for 15 days in consequence. He left one son, Victor Amedee, who carried on his title of Prince of Carignan. The deaf Emmanuel Philbert is an ancestor, in direct line, of the Italian Kings beginning with King Victor Emmanuel who was crowned in 1861.

In the Savoy region where the deaf Prince governed, there was, without doubt, some 100 or so people similarly afflicted as the Prince and he could not have failed to know of their existence. But to the gentry they were termed as poor and boorish. This term probably influenced Emmanuel Philbert since no records revealed any contact with them or attempt to succour them. Had he been a compassionate man he could easily have done something to ease their plight, perhaps by offering facilities for their education or given them employment on his vast estates.

Educating the Deaf in France, Britain and Beyond

Chapter Three

Following the success of Pedro Ponce de Leon, Juan Pablo Bonet and Manuel Ramirez de Carrion in Spain, it became known and accepted that the Deaf can be educated and dumb taught to speak. From 1616 to the end of the 18th century, books on instructions for the Deaf came to light from the pens of G Bonifacio (1616), Bonet (1620), John Bulwer (1648), John Wallis (1653), George Dalgarno (1661 & 1680), DuVerney (1693), Dr Johann Ammon (1700), Samuel Heinicke (1755), Charles Michel Abbé del'Epée (1755 & 1776), Pastor Arnoldi (1777) and Abbé Roche-Ambroise Siccard (1782). Most of the writers dealt with the teaching of speech and reading lips which was later to make a worldwide impact and subject unwilling deaf children to acquire hearing people's mode of communication and to be severely punished if they fail.

The first recorded free school for the Deaf was established in Paris by Abbé de l'Epée in 1755 and in 1760 Thomas Braidwood opened a school for paying Deaf pupils in Edinburgh.

Charles Michel Abbé de l'Epée was born in 1712 into a wealthy family. His father was an architect in the Sun King Louis XIV's service at Versailles. He studied for priesthood but was refused permission to take holy vows as he declined to sign an oath abjuring the heretical teachings of Jansenism. He turned to legal studies and was admitted to the Paris bar. Later he returned to his religious calling and a lenient bishop gave him a small canonry at Troyes where he was ordained priest. He lost his post when a new bishop of the diocese displaced him with one of his friends. Epée returned to Paris with a burning desire to do good, living on a modest allowance from his family. He frequented poorer quarters and on one such visit, he encountered two deaf twin sisters who were obviously born deaf and communicated only by crude gestures, perhaps of their own making. This dramatic moment led him to take up the education of those who have been outcasts ever since.

Epée's earlier involvement in philosophical studies caused him to doubt the Augustine theory that faith comes through the ear. He asserted that the written word can give the Deaf knowledge of God. Sign language was in existence long before Epée came to the scene but at the time it was difficult to be sure that it was possible to cover abstract substance so he thought about the hand signs for every letter of the language which was tried in Spain but found wanting. He perfected a dactylogy, better known as the manual alphabet, thus enabling his pupils to spell out words in grammatical French. The alphabet showing one-hand finger signs can be seen to this above the tomb where he lies buried in the crypt of the little church, Saint-Roch, in Rue St Honore, Paris. This monument credits Epée as the perpetuator of the one-handed manual alphabet which was later to be adopted worldwide.

Epée had 26 pupils when his school was at its height. Reading and writing was the main theme but he also gave exercises in other languages such as Italian, Latin and Spanish. His pupils responded to questions about baptism and penitence in French as well as in the other languages. Later, English and German were added. "Why several languages?" was a question put to him. He answered that it was to show the world that the Deaf educated following his method could rearrange their thoughts to different grammars, whatever their national language. This was obviously to show the superiority of his method over others particularly oral instruction which had gained preference especially by parents who do not wish their Deaf children to be using a different mode of communication to their own. Such parents, mostly wealthy, found their own champion in the person of Jacob Rodrigues Pereire who successfully educated their children by oral means, using signing only as an accessory. He won widespread acclaim which reached the ears of Louis XV who granted him annual funding to continue in his role as an instructor. Pereire and Epée clashed over means of teaching and Pereire accused Epée of filling his school with pariahs in order to gain sympathy from society and royalty. This was the first historical clash which was later to lead to the long standing controversy over the oral versus manual means of educating Deaf children.

Charles-Michel del'Epée had another adversary in the person of Samuel Heinicke (1723- 1790). Influenced by Amman of Amsterdam, who published a book on education by oral means similar to Bonet's, Heinicke started to teach a few Deaf children of wealthy families. Later he was invited to open a school at Leipzig on the invitation of Frederick Augustus, Prince of Saxony. It started in 1778 with 9 pupils and was the first school for the Deaf in Germany. Like Epée, he made sure that the pupils were from poor families so that he could consider himself justified in accepting the prince's funding. His main task was to make the pupils speak and understand what was spoken but in cases of difficulties, which were rife, he resorted to sign language. He and Epée got to know of each other and exchanged letters denouncing each other's methods to teaching the Deaf and the systems used. Heinicke wrote an eulogy on speech, claiming it to be God's gift and he ludicrously asserted that abstract concepts were possible only through the voice. This gave Epée vent to attack him and brand him a charlatan. Epée's argument was that too much reliance on articulation did not help mental development. The German governing bodies, however, believed that their countryman was on the right tracks and they gave him support. Teachers destined to teach the Deaf were sent to be trained under him. Thus the foundation of the German System of Deaf education was established without forethought of the disservice it was to herald.

Epée fed the pupils, paid the salaries of his assistants and the upkeep of the school from his inheritance. After his death in 1789 the school continued and a successor was found in the person of Abbé Roch-Ambroise Sicard, who was connected with the Bordeaux School for the Deaf which opened about 1786. Louis XVI confirmed Sicard's appointment and had earlier ordered funds to be provided for the running of the school. As the number of pupils increased, the funds were insufficient and did not provide the necessities of life. It was left to Sicard to plead before the Committee on Mendicancy of the National Assembly. He succeeded and the school was transferred to a Celestine monastery, later named St Jacques, and was declared a national establishment thus qualifying for permanent funding.

The Braidwood Academy probably originated in Scotland when a born deaf boy, Charles Sheriff, son of a prosperous Leith merchant was introduced to Thomas Braidwood for lessons in reading and writing. Braidwood became interested in the boy's affliction and tried to teach him speech. Having started to teach the Deaf, he made it his life's work. The school was established at a house in St Leonard's Hill, Edinburgh, later known as Dumbiedykes Road which still exists. Braidwood took paying pupils and his foremost task was speech teaching and lipreading and in addition there was "talking hands" that presumably meant the two-handed alphabet recorded by the father of communication theory, George Dalgarno of Aberdeen. It is thought that he regarded this as an alternative means to writing. However, evidence shows that he did not adhere to the mechanical learning of words by rote. "The attention of the teacher should be ever on the watch to seize, and, as far as possible, to create suitable occasions for the exemplification of his lessons." Furthermore, "The same examples and illustrations will by no means suit all learners, and the teacher who should depend upon such general instruction will find himself miserably deceived."

These remarks published elsewhere show that Braidwood deeply understood the education of the Deaf but he declined to reveal anything connected with his methods of instructing. They were close guarded secrets and were no help to Deaf children who parents were unable to afford his fees. What of these children at the time and soon afterwards? There is a slight historical evidence to indicate that some parents attempted to teach their Deaf offspring to speak and write their native language, leading to self-teaching later on. Quite a few succeeded but research failed to reveal any exceptional cases who made some impact on literacy circles. Apart from "talking hands", Braidwood had another "secret weapon" which he failed to conceal from leakage. It was a small round piece of silver, a few inches long, the size of a tobacco pipe, flattened at one end with a ball as large as a marble at the other. It was placed on the pupil's tongue as a means to correct the tongue's position for the articulation of different vowels and consonants. Speech teaching involved the teacher to use many facial distortions and grimaces to show the pupil the positions and actions of several organs. The pupil was expected to follow suit. Several were sickened by this exercise which was later to cause a storm of protest.

Nevertheless, the Academy was widely reported to be successful. Some of its pupils were distinguished and showed realism of high aspirations. Such were F G McKenzie, a MP, who later became a colonial Governor General and later moved to the House of Lords as Lord Seaforth, J P Wood, a senior civil servant who wrote the biography of John Law of Lauriston and last but not least, John Goodricke, perhaps the most influential Deaf intellectual in history, whose carefully scientific astronomy laid the foundations of all modern measurement and hence theories about the entire universe and whose genius gained him the membership of the Royal Society at the age of 21. Goodricke College at York University is probably the only university residential college to be named after a born, profoundly Deaf person.

Dr Samuel Johnson got to hear of the Academy and he came to visit it with his companion, James Boswell. Hitherto Johnson regarded deaf-mutism a ghastly horror but what he saw at the school astonished him and he was able to hold short conversations orally with some of the pupils. Johnson's writing about the experience commenting on the pupils' ability to read, write and speak well, gave the expression that they "hear with the eye". Another 18th century writer, William Pennant, also gave supportive evidence and together, the 2 writers ensured the school's reputation throughout the Continent. Braidwood's profession was passed down to his son, John, and nephew, Thomas Watson. They set up schools in London, Brighton and the USA.

The most revered educator according to historical recordings and comments by Deaf activists is Charles-Michel Abbé de l'Epée. It was probably because of the system through which he imparted instructions so easily understood by most of his pupils. During his lifetime, no sketches of the Abbé were in evidence although there was artistic potential among his students. The Abbé had refused any representation of himself to be made till the appearance of Claude-Andre Deseine (1740-1823). Deseine was 20 and unschooled but he was already a working sculptor when he appeared at the Abbe's school just as it opened in 1760 to be educated. Deseine made designs of the Abbe's features in secret by helping in the mass and memorising when in close contact. He executed a bust based on these

21

designs and it was revealed in 1786, 3 years before the Abbe's death. It was the only lifelike portrayal of the Abbé left to posterity from which other artists made copies. At the base of the bust he wrote a poem about the marvellous secret his teacher revealed that is talking by hands and hearing by the eyes. The bust was then donated to the National Institution of the Deaf, Paris. Claude-Andre Deseine was the son of a Paris joiner. Out of a family of 15 children, only 6 reached maturity of whom 4 were artistically gifted. The best known, Louis-Pierre, an Academician of Paris, was the sculptor to Prince of Condé and winner of the Grand Prix of Rome in 1780. His brother, Louis-Etienne, a talented architect, died at the age of 32. Their sister, Madeleine-Anne, was a competent painter and designer. The last of the gifted 4, Claude-Andre was Deaf from birth and some of his works, signed by himself, carried the title of "Deseine, Deaf Mute." His works won him a number of distinctions and gained him entry into the Academie Royale at the age of 35 as a pupil of the sculptor Pajou. When he was 40 he began to exhibit in Paris salons and achieved a considerable reputation. He was commissioned to make a posthumous bust of Danton's first wife - a macabre task which necessitated the exhumation of the lady's body 7 days after burial.

Deseine was well cared and loved by his father but on the death of the parent in 1777 he was declared by law to be incapable of managing his affairs by reason of deafness and his younger brother, Louis-Pierre, was appointed trustee over him. It was not till 1868 when Ferdinand Berthier in his Code Napoleon attacked the ruling as a breach of human rights especially in the case of a talented artist who had given France a treasured collection.

In 1823, the trusteeship had developed on a nephew and the old sculptor was living in poverty in a lodging house on the outskirts of the city. He petitioned the Government for assistance declaring that he deserved well of the State because of his work in the field of the arts and pointing out that previous governments had granted him aid in times of need. In the petition, he stated himself as unemployed, old, infirm and abandoned despite being one of the most famous sculptors of the Republic who works had benefitted ministries and authorities. no reply was received and a few months afterwards Deseine had died.

C.A. Deseine and his creation, the bust
of Abbé de l'Epée

During the 18th century, Britain had no system of education under state control.
The education of lower classes were left entirely to voluntary agencies who
provided charity schools, Sunday schools, small Private schools and Dame schools
- not for the very poorest children and these did not cater for Deaf children. The
great idea was to provide the poor with such education as would not make them
discontented with their lot in life but make them as Dickens wrote:-

> "To love their occupations,
> Bless the squire and his relations,
> Live upon their daily rations,
> And always know their proper stations."

It is remarkable how neglect and abuses were allowed to continue, often for long periods, without protest and looked upon as if providence had ordained them until some pioneer starts an agitation for their removal. The pioneer is usually rewarded by being denounced as an infidel and malcontent and treated like a heretic.

It 1803, a Bill was introduced in the House of Commons to establish a system of rate-aided parochial schools but was rejected by the House of Lords. After this, controversy arose over a system of unsectarian education introduced by Joseph Lancaster, a Quaker, who was extraordinarily successful in establishing a number of schools. A feature of this system was the "monitorial method" that was employing the more advanced pupils to teach the less advanced, a method that continued in schools for many years. The success of Lancaster's activity stirred the Anglican Church to counter it. By 1811, the Church was so far successful that it was able to found "The National Society for promoting the Education of the poor in the principles of the Established Church of England, throughout England and Wales." The movement spread quickly and its object was avowedly to secure the predominance of the influence of the Church in popular education. Subscriptions flowed in and a charge of one penny a week was made in most schools. However, "The British and Foreign School Society" was formed in 1814 to take over Lancaster's ventures including a teacher training school in London. The motive behind these rival movements was to exclude state interference in education.

The Reform Bill of 1832 extending the franchise and giving a wider representation of the people had an almost immediate result, for the first Parliamentary Grant towards the cost of Elementary Education was made in 1833. The Grant was low but the small beginning was welcomed by advanced educationist as evidence that the Government had entered on a new policy from which future Governments would not dare depart.

The Church of England became alarmed lest unsectarian religious education might be introduced so it obtained a concession for the introduction of school inspectors approved by the Archbishop.

The Slow Dawning of Enlightenment

Chapter Four

Towards the end of the 18th century evidence abounded to show that the Deaf can be educated and with this thought in mind, the old Aristotle and Augustine philosophies lost their credibility. Among the educated classes, at least, they were ceasing to be the butts and objects of contempt and their affliction a joke. This was due to the realisation that something could be done to relieve them of their misery. Fatalism was yielding to the feelings of mercy and pity, as the way of a more hopeful mind. Men are most biased in the presence of evil beyond their understanding or control. All this thinking begot humanitarian fervour that led to the formation of movements to provide education for Deaf children from poor families. This resulted in the appearance of institutions and asylums in a number of major British cities at the turn of the century. Their existence depended solely on voluntary contributions and in order to get this subsistence, stress was made upon religious education which these so-called schools were enforced to provide.

"Help the Deaf to Know God" was widely used as an appeal and this induced people to give alms. The thought of any human being not knowing God was appalling at the time. Time and energy was spent upon the several means of unloosening the purse-strings of the wealthy.

Asylums of the time meant shelter from the harshness of the world. The poorest Deaf children were admitted but they turned out to be little devils with horrible habits and barbarous noises. This was the result of them being unable to comprehend parental commands, generally given by voice. Parents who used gestures had better behaved children. Teachers had to be hard and sometimes cruel to control them but who dare criticise them? It was noted that the less robust families of the population were susceptible to infections which were passed on to their children thus causing deafness or other disabling diseases. In this respect, most Deaf children came from poor families. Amazingly good essays supposed to be the children's work were produced. Had they been genuine they would have put modern teaching results to shame. But they were forged in that fashion because that was what the patrons expected asylum children to write. A steady income depended on passing the whole thing off as a modern miracle.

The asylums or instituted schools were little better than the workhouses described by Dickens. The trend was to make them self-supporting by making the pupils work in the garden, laundry, cookhouse and workshops involving carpentry, tailoring, dressmaking, bootmaking and printing. Priests took an interest in these establishments, having done so much in the name of Christ, and yet allowed their work to continue in the narrowest interpretation of His teachings. They were so concerned with the rationalist threat to faith and morals that they shut the best ideas from the minds of the children. Small children sometimes had to endure three hours in church and not hearing a word from the pulpit or a note of the music.

Religious education was given a degree of importance in the school curriculum as it proved to be a means of raising voluntary contributions from the well to do and it also satisfied the clergy who kept prying in the affairs of schools. English was essential to read the scriptures so the two subjects went hand in hand. Several pupils approaching school leaving age were successful and sometimes they were allowed to deputise for absent teachers but one had to be sure that these children were well versed in the scriptures and behave impeccably. They were the ones destined to become leaders of the Deaf in adult life but unfortunately the narrow teaching did not broaden their minds towards getting rid of paternalism and establishing the society of Deaf people as an independent body with full access to civil rights and allowed decision making in the areas that concerned them.

Dependence of funds from affluent and influential people, an overpowering essential, induced these people to request a say in the management and to refuse them some role would have been asking for trouble. This would have threatened the flow of income. So here beget paternalism which was the curse of the Deaf community for more than a century.

On the completion of schooling there emanated the desire to congregate and meet others in like condition, especially those who, like themselves, use the language of signs. The initiative in founding such societies or community groups was generally taken by Deaf individuals possessing superior education or financial means who endeavour to ameliorate the condition of their less fortunate brethren. The first recorded congregation took place in 1818 when a group of Deaf men met just to have a talk at the corner of Lawnmarket and Bank Street in Edinburgh where stands the notorious Deacon Brodie's Tavern. A Miss Elizabeth Burnside, a well to do resident of the city noted them and she obtained a room for them, paid the rent and acted as the doorkeeper. Later with the help of the principal of the Edinburgh Deaf Institute, the place become known as Edinburgh Deaf and Dumb Meeting. In 1822, John Anderson, believed to be Deaf, held religious services in his own house. Endowed with some degree of education, having a trade and involved in the society of Deaf people, it came as no surprise when this group launched a publication. The first known magazine appeared in 1843 under the title of The Edinburgh Messenger. It made only twelve appearances before disappearing, no doubt due to lack of funds and poor circulation. In later years, others cropped up and most of the contributions came from Deaf writers. The quality of the writings was quite high and it appeared that most of the writers aspired to write like Dickens whose novels were the most widely read at the time. These old publications displayed evidence that the Deaf were adequately educated and some managed to attain a high standard.

Institution schools and missions for the Deaf increased as time went by and by the end of the 19th century, there were 95 certified schools catering for 3123 pupils in Britain. About 500 existed in the world by 1895. Queen Victoria, who took a personal interest in the Deaf and was able to use the manual alphabet efficiently, found out that only one existed in India at Bombay when the country had about 150,000 known Deaf people. She made a plea for more schools to be opened in the country.

The Dark Ages of Oralism

Chapter Five

"We have ways of making you talk"

In 1975, a pile of papers were found in a New York dustbin. They were dated 1845 and written by Rev. Day whose relative had a Deaf child which led him to take an interest in methods of educating the Deaf. He was gifted with a sharp nose and tireless legs and these attributions led him to pry into the affairs of schools and institutions engaged in giving instruction to Deaf children and adults. He toured Europe and came to Germany where he found education of the Deaf a real horror. German teachers had an unwavering belief that the Deaf can be made to speak and their efforts towards that goal were relentless. They contorted their faces to exaggeration in exhibiting the positions of the tongue, teeth and lips that made themselves unpleasant to look at. Slow learners had their tongues grabbed and a ruler forced in their mouths to manipulate the tongue into making the required movement. These hapless pupils strained themselves, particularly their lungs, from early morning to late evening. Many succumbed to consumption through lung strain. Out of a total of 20 pupils at the Leipzig School for the Deaf, 17 were victims of the disease which at the time was a killer and most of them died.

This type of education, which was really an enforcement of a means of communication rather than imparting knowledge, became known as the German Method. Since its aim was to give Deaf children speech, a course supposed to lead to normality as compared to abnormality which the signing Deaf people appear to be branded with. This German Method won widespread approval particularly among parents of Deaf children, teachers and educators in Germany. It gathered momentum and efforts were made to influence other countries. In France, Britain, Spain and USA, where the Deaf were educated in sign language, there was ample evidence that attainments in education were subject to encouragement and there were glowing reports on some pupils' progress. Much of the evidence lies in Deaf adults' writings in their respective country's language which have been left for posterity. Some old magazines published for or by the Deaf which have survived show a high standard of written language. On the other hand, very few comparable writings from oralist Germany are in existence so it is in no way possible to credit the way the Germans educated their Deaf children.

Nevertheless, the Germans were and still are persuasive people. History reveals that their handling of propaganda was masterly. From the second half of the 19th century, the German Method gospel was given elaborate appeal even to exaggerations. Even untruths were not spared. Such allurement most naturally gained sympathisers from the public who could understand only spoken language and detest any means to substitute it. This led to one of the worst forms of deception that occurred in 1880.

Since the education of the Deaf was given under two different instructions, the German and French methods, the latter derived from Abbé del'Epée, favoured sign language and the two led to much controversy, some very caustic and injurious to Deaf children who were used in experiments to prove the merits of either. It was felt for some time that there should be some discussion among the experts, thus leading to an agreement upon which system to recommend. In theory, the idea was commendable but how it was achieved was most degrading.

For some years prior to 1880, the Pereire Society which was established in France and which fanatically supported the pure oral system and wanted a total ban imposed on sign language, got professionals engaged in the education of the Deaf interested in holding a congress to discuss recommendations on education. The Society owed its foundation to a wealthy banking family that agreed to finance the congress on one condition, namely, the carriage of an overwhelming vote in favour of the oral system and condemnation of sign language. The Society had no problem as to who should be chosen as delegates to the congress, as it kept records of teachers, educators and authorities supporting its cause.

The congress finally got under way at Milan from 6th to 11th September and there were 158 delegates, 83 Italian, 56 French, 9 English, 5 American, 3 Swedish, 1 Belgian and only one German. The strange thing was only one from Germany, the bastion of pure oralism. This was to eliminate what would very obviously term the conference as biased. But the 83 from Italy were either strong supporters of the German System or were forced to embrace it by the fear of losing their jobs, mostly in teaching. Some of the delegates were known opponents of the rigidity of a single system of instruction and they favoured the combined system which used speech and sign language simultaneously. But they were powerful people who were heads of large schools and to keep them out would only invite adverse criticism. Nevertheless, they were in the minority and when the conference started on 6th September, everyone knew there would be no defeat for the oral system.

At the start of the meeting, a small number of pupils from the Milan and Como schools for the Deaf were brought in. They were carefully selected and none of them went Deaf before the age of 7 so all had normal speech. Some had useful residual hearing and others exceptional lipreading skills. 46 of the delegates came from these 2 schools and some of them tested the pupils before the assembly, asking questions and getting correct orally given answers. Deaf historian, Albert Ballin, called them "decoys". When the stage-managed farce ended the assembly gave a standing ovation. Some thought oralism was the most wonderful thing for deafdom. No one dared to rise and ask about pupils not so well endowed as the few, as this was known as a surefire invitation to black looks.

Speeches that were given were mostly one-sided, eulogising the means that give Deaf children speech, then mastery of their native language that was supposed to follow. One delegate spoke of speech being God-given that promotes thought and ideas and of signing as devil-inspired, breeding nonsense. Unanimous among the supporters of oralism was the belief that sign language could not cover abstract phenomenon although at the time there was a paper in circulation written by a Deaf intellectual, Henri Gaillard, that gave ample evidence that anything abstract can be expounded in sign language. Delegates were asked to ignore it and to try and expose the writer as a charlatan.

The Rev Dr Thomas Gallaudet, Rector of St Ann's Church for the Deaf, New York, pleaded for the combined system and he was allowed to give a version of the Lord's Prayer in sign language that was elaborate and expressive. Some listened while others turned their faces away in disgust, thus betraying traces of near-paranoid prejudice among the assembly.

A London medical man, E Symes-Thompson, MD, FRCP, of Brompton Chest Hospital, delivered a paper on the health of deaf mutes. He attacked the non-speaking Deaf for endangering the health of their lungs. He noticed that consumption among Deaf mutes was proportionally higher than among normal people. He also noticed that they breathe through the mouth instead of the nose thus making themselves susceptible to epilepsy, various head affections, discharge from the ears giving off an offensive odour and chilblains. Deaf people trained to speak on the other hand, he remarked, appeared to be free from any of the symptoms mentioned and they lived longer than the dumb. He concluded that all Deaf people must be made to speak for their own benefit in health and education. The doctor was thunderously applauded.

On 7th September, a resolution declaring that the oral method ought to be preferred to that of signs for the education and instruction of the Deaf and dumb was put to vote. Those in favour numbered 160, the number included the president, vice-president and other non- delegate officials. The dissentients were only 4. The topmost issue had yet to come and this crucial point, to which the supporters of the oral system looked with undisguised enthusiasm, took place at the end of the meeting on 9th September. It was stressed that sign language was a disadvantage, injuring speech, lipreading and the precision of ideas. Voting by a majority of about 150 to 16, passed a declaration that sign language should be discouraged, in real meaning, banned in all schools for the Deaf. This was a victory for the instigators of the congress, the Pereire Society and its backers. Under the pretext of giving speech to Deaf children, the Congress obtained by guile sanction to ban sign language.

31

To deny the Deaf a language that is coherent to them is an ultimate transgression of human rights. It denies them an ingenious means of expressing themselves with ease and clarity and attempts to turn them into imperfect and very sorry imitations of a hearing person, thus subjecting them to greater ridicule.

The Congress termed as International Congress on the Education of the Deaf ended in a fanfare of triumph. It was argued that it was never international or representative as reporters, observers, particularly Deaf people were barred from it. It was entirely in the hands of a party inflamed with the spirit of conquest seeking for the present victory of a vote rather than the tardier triumph that might follow unimpassioned discussion and the simple presentation of facts and results. The 5 American delegates, led by Dr Edward Miner Gallaudet and Dr Harvey Peet who represented more than 6,000 pupils and who preferred the combined system to the rigid oral approach, never had their papers recorded as the Congress chairman, Abba Tarra, declared that they were in the minority and their counsels fully rejected. Deaf delegates were in an even greater minority. In fact, the only 2 Deaf delegates were Claudius Forestier, director of the Lyon School for the Deaf and J Denison, the American who accompanied Dr Gallaudet. Nevertheless, the Treaty of Milan, 1880, was created and its resolutions published and distributed to all known schools that were in existence. Later on, when Deaf people and their sympathisers got to know about the ignominy, the Treaty became known as the Infamous Treaty.

The declarations were printed impressively and sent to all existing schools for the Deaf in an effort to impose oralism and to stamp out sign language. Half the number of schools immediately responded. Children were ordered not to sign and those who disobeyed, more through habit than defiance, were forced to sit upon their hands and in stubborn cases, they had their hands tied behind their backs. Enforcing them to speak was brought to the extreme and pupils who apparently suffered as a result were dealt with unsympathetically and given scoldings by their teachers. It was exasperation on one side and misery on the other. Deaf teachers who were doing well and in many cases, better than their hearing counterparts through sharing a common problem with their charges, were regarded as a stumbling block to the imposition of the oral system and they were given the sack from their jobs. Mostly, they received no compensation or commend for their success, particularly in their paving the way for their pupils towards acquiring literacy.

This demonic treatment did not go along without rousing sympathy. Dr Heidsieck, a teacher at the Weissenfels School for the Deaf, Germany, regarded the treatment as atrocious and failing as an educational tool. He argued that oral language was meant for the ear and attempts to make the Deaf appreciate it through the eye is a violation of nature. He remonstrated against the directors and masters of the institution but to no effect. His fellow teachers, fearing the loss of their livelihood as in what happened to the Deaf teachers, refused to side with him. The pupils to had no power to make their wrongs known and if they did, they knew that life would be more intolerable than before. So most of them found it sensible to remain silent but there were former pupils who were now liberated from fear and 147 of them, mostly from the Breslau and Altwasser areas, together with their hearing relatives and other educated Deaf people in other areas, signed a petition instigated by Dr Heidsieck. It had 800 signatures, together with a lengthy letter giving evidence of abuses, and was sent to Emperor William on 24th November 1891. It was passed to a Herr Bosse, who at the time was Minister of Clerical, Educational and Medical Affairs, for his verdict. It was obvious that he never met a Deaf person or knew of the problems common to the Deaf but he knew all about the Treaty of Milan. His reply contained such remarks as no small number of distinguished and gifted men, at times with great sacrifice, and rare zeal devoted their best energies to provide Deaf children with the heavenly gift of speech (How on earth has it to be taught if it is a gift from Heaven?) He went on to say that speech prevents their severance from their families in which they were born, the church to which they belong and the State whose protection that may claim. Such arrogance and downright ignorance gave him no valid reason to change the oral method of instruction for the Deaf or to take steps to persecute teachers for cruelty towards their charges.

The Bosse letter was dated September 17th 1892, and a copy was sent to the Weissenfels Institution where the directors met and immediately issued a writ for slander against Dr Heidsieck. The good doctor, on an act of mercy, was ironically exposed in the court as a liar and troublemaker and was fined a nominal sum. He lost his job and the high cost his lawyer's fee precipitated him into a stage of financial embarrassment. However, his friends and sympathisers in Germany, England and America opened a fund to alleviate his state. Nothing more was heard of him towards the turn of the century, by which time, sign language in all German schools for the Deaf was completely eliminated. A number of schools in other countries, particularly English speaking, tried the oral system and found that it did not benefit the pupils educationally so they retained the well tried system combining speech and sign language.

In France, the oral system that was imposed was the result of the whim of one man, the Minister of Public Instruction, who at the time had a massive hold in the jurisdiction governing schools. Teachers, finding oralism a failure or defect, preferred to remain silent for fear of offending the minister. Any offending teacher ran the risk of getting the sack.

In Britain from 1887 to 1896, Governments hesitated in passing the Elementary Education Bill for the Deaf and Blind. The vociferous elements supporting the Milan Treaty dictation failed to touch Members of Parliament. Most of them were wary of the claims that Deaf people with speech that was anything but intelligible, could be made to talk. The State was really indifferent to the Deaf. The attitude was still that of the 1889 report which classified the Deaf and Blind with idiots and imbeciles. When the idea of training special qualified teachers for the Deaf was discussed, up cropped the question of the need of such teachers for useless children.

The 1907 Act brought into being the Medical Branch of the Board of Education under Dr Eicholz. A Medical inspection revealed a much greater extent of deafness among children but by putting education of Deaf children under medical control, the effect of the Act was to continue bias against the Deaf. Teachers were aggrieved but there was not sufficient pressure to end the absurdity of medical control of educational matters. Most doctors of the time had never met a Deaf person, never knew anything about the implication of deafness and the culture of the Deaf. The Deaf themselves made no effort to protest. The educated ones who could have remonstrated were in most cases highly religious and they accepted their fate as a human misfortune and destined themselves to the will of God. The few who revolted failed to gain backing so their attempts to ferment indignation floundered and died out.

In early 20th century, there were Deaf children whose lives were not more than shuttling to and fro between the Poor Law Institution and the Deaf Institution. There were 14,000 Deaf children known to be without a place in a school. Their right to education was made law only as recently as 1918, the result of recommendations made by Edward Wood, President of the Board of Education.

Not all professions were so unkind and uncaring however, and schools for the Deaf in London became known to drivers of cabs, buses and trams who were careful to keep a wary eye so as not to injure any children during the beginning and ending of school hours.

A German researcher, commenting upon his country's insistence on the oral system of education during the 20th century, gave the view that it became unrealistic in its goal, resulting in society having distorted views of people regarded as "the others" who try to emulate the hearing. Such an attitude, the researcher stated, has strong resemblance to racism and anti-semitism, prevalent prejudices in this country for many years. On the other hand, those who have no shame in their deafness and act as the ones with a sign language background, seem to be better tolerated by society.

35

Cinderella Strikes Back

Chapter Six

The lack of historical evidence that refers to the lives of ordinary Deaf people prior to the 18th century is a serious drawback in providing a representation of how they managed to exist and overcome the odds stacked against them in an uncaring society. However, research reveals that Cinderella like exploitation of Deaf people was practised especially in using them as employees. From the Middle Ages up to the present day, Deaf workers are hired on condition that they accept a low wage and agree to partake in work, usually repetitive, which ordinary workers would shun. One asked his employer why he was not paid the same rate as others for the same kind of work. The abrupt reply was "Because you are deaf." Where there is muck-raking to be done, the immediate move was to give it to the Deaf one who lacks the means to complain or refuse through fear of losing his employ. This was the general expectation Deaf workers were subject to but not all complied. There were some whose intelligence and trade skills were significant. They went their own way and became successful business people and found ways of dealing with clients despite their handicap. A street still in existence at Funchal on the Portuguese island of Madeira known as RUA DO SORD. Translated it means "Road of the Deaf". According to legend, it had shops, particularly workshops, on both sides and a number of them were ran or owned by Deaf trade people, engaged on bootmaking, carpentry, carving, tailoring, printing and painting. The Portuguese nobility and wealthy had their overseas retreat on the island. A marked lack of craft service led to immigration of craftsmen among which were some Deaf artisans. Those workers proved to be excellent and reliable and were much in demand. When they died, their hearing heirs took over and created a change that diminished the crafts. The street's name stands to record the type of people who commanded respect in trading.

Beyond Europe, the status of Deaf people was usually low and their treatment dire to desperate. Even employing Deaf mutes was a form of folly to most people of bygone eras but the intelligence of a despot found a use for some of them but in a damning manner. In the 17th century, Murad, Sultan of Ottoman Empire, died leaving 103 children. The eldest succeeded him and became Sultan Muhamad III. His 19 brothers were soon involved in a plot to oust him from the throne and share it among themselves. It came to Muhamad's notice and he had them all seized and thrown into a huge jail which he eventually built in the Seraglio in Constantinople. He knew that jailers with promises of wealth are easily bribed so he recruited strong men without hearing, speech and education to be his brothers' guardians and all attempts at bribery floundered.

The accolade of the first Deaf man in history to start a riot is credited to Umai of Tinnevelly, a region in the Southern tip of Indian. Around 1760/1770, the federal chiefs in the area, known as the Poligars, objected to paying taxes to the British and wanted independence. A rebellion was started by the Poligar of Tinnevelly and his 3 sons, the youngest one being Umai which in Hindi means Dumb Brother. In 1799, British troops were sent to quell this revolt that led to a 3 month long war. Umai was completely Deaf and used only sign language. The gestures he used were most spectacular and vivid to the crowds that gathered around him. As a rabble rouser of exceptional forte he inflamed a few thousand desperadoes into taking on the whole might of the British Empire. In October, of the year the revolt was crushed, the Poligar hanged and his 3 sons were imprisoned. In February 1801, Umai escaped and gathered 5,000 men to continue the rebellion. They occupied a fort and held out against 3,000 British troops. It took 2 months to storm the fort. Umai and his remaining 2,000 men continued the war outside the fort which lasted 4 months. It ended when Umai was eventually captured and hanged like a common felon. He was a ferocious warrior and was worshipped by his men. In his memoirs, the British commander, General Walsh, mentioned that Umai was one of the most extraordinary mortals he had ever known.

This man, so severely handicapped by deprivation of voice, a faculty so high in importance for leaders of men, found an effective alternative. The moral to be drawn from this outstanding example is "Never underestimate the power of the fanatic and the far-reaching possibilities of a visual language."

There were still some parts in the world where respect is accorded to Deaf people and their language. The most notable was Martha's Vineyard, off the coast of Massachusetts in USA. Anthropologist Nora Ellen Grove in her book "Everyone Here Spoke Sign Language" records such a large concentration of Deaf people on the island during the 18th and 19th centuries. The islanders were close-knit and they married among themselves and through blood relationship they begot Deaf children. Further intermarriages caused "Deaf" genes to increase. In the hamlet of Chilmark which had a population of 500 in 1880, there were 20 who were Deaf mutes, thus recording the very high incidence rate of 1 in 25. By weight of the number of Deaf people, the hearing became bilingual, using speech and sign language. None of them would have dreamed of using speech when there were one or more Deaf people present. Sign language simultaneously used with speech was common at gatherings and church services. Here Deaf people knew no discriminations, so rife elsewhere, and many of them took an active role in town meetings and civic affairs. By being able to communicate with almost everyone, their widely known handicap was minimal and problems few. For the Deaf this type of society was ideal. Before the turn of the 19th century, the inhabitants flocked to the mainland where salaries were higher and married mainlanders. "Deaf" genes, as a result, died out and deafness faded but the island's legend remains.

An almost identical community has for centuries and still is going strong among the Amazonian tribe, Urubu-Kaaport, in Brazil. Their tradition of intramarriage has produced a large number of Deaf natives. The hearing, enforced by the need to communicate with their Deaf fellow beings, took to the use of sign language and some of them found great convenience in its use even with those who were not Deaf. According to evidence, the tribe appear content with their lot and shunned any ventures into the outside speech dominated world.

The Masasi tribe of Tanzania is another one in similar circumstances but very little record has been made of them. Their language is known as Chari-Nile.

"How about a deaf-mute colony, a kingdom of our own?" signed John J Flournoy around the middle of the 19th century in America. Hats hit the air when he delivered an account in acquiring government land for a self-existing community where all citizens would be Deaf and the chief means of communication would be sign language. He also supported the idea of having its own representative in the Congress and he stated his willingness to be considered as one of the candidates. Trade with the outside world could be done by the hearing children of Deaf parents by acting as ambassadors. He felt that the community would flourish and become wealthy as most Deaf people at the time were skilled craftsmen and not subject to exploitation by greedy employers. Those who came to listen felt there was sense in the project but Flournoy's closest friend, Edmund Booth, threw cold water over it. He argued that after a few generations, the colony would become non-existent because a very small percentage of the offsprings of Deaf parents are Deaf. All attempts at segregation were doomed to fail. His view suggests that the Deaf are compelled to take the painful and frustrating path to integrate into the hearing world even if it means adopting second or lower class citizenship.

But second class citizenship forms no part of the experience of Gallaudet University, the Deaf enclave in the very heart of the capital of the USA. And a more positive, more recent version of the Vineyard model was aired in Bulgaria in 1979 (Holmes 1980).

"In Israel, the Jews replaced the Ghetto with the Kibbutz, the stigmatised with the admired. Why are deaf communities often compared with the Ghetto but not the Kibbutz? Perhaps the founding of a Deaf homeland, approved by the United Nations, would solve many problems.

So we propose the founding of Surdica, capital city of Surdania, homeland of the Deaf of the world. Here all hospitals, schools, colleges, police, courts and government are run by the Deaf majority and their families with full citizenship rights accorded to the hearing minority. Surdania would be sighted near the overlap of Africa, Europe and Asia where the Mediterranean climate is conducive to gesticulation gloves and mittens being unnecessary. The climate would also suit the massive influx of Deaf immigrants, partial immigrants, guest workers, students, tourists and the large numbers of Deaf people who would choose to spend their retirement in this duty-free communication haven.

But Utopias are still susceptible to plumbing problems and let us call a halt before we get involved in minutiae. Let us, instead return to the aftermath of comment precipitated by our paper, or rather to the main result of this which has been to crystallise our views into what has come to be known as "The Bulgarian Thesis" or more accurately "The Bulgarian Dialectic". This states:

A **Thesis** Integration as cooperation is the ideal solution to deafness.
B **Antithesis** Integration as assimilation is the final solution to deafness.
C **Synthesis** Only a genocidal dastard would prefer B to A."

Kill or Cure

Chapter Seven

The congenital Deaf or victims of deafness acquired in early childhood appear unconcerned about being bereft of hearing. It is their parents who undergo traumatic discomfort. Communication problems cloud their minds and being without speech, the resultant accompaniment of deafness, is frightening. The first question that crops up in their minds is that which has always came readily to parents of afflicted children "Is there a cure?" Never in history has there been a negative response. The list of charlatans from the cradle of history to the present day is far too long to record. Parents tormented by worry find themselves seeking their service and listening to their claims, sometimes unbelievably absurd. It was always thought that deafness was merely a blockage of the ears so all crude forms of penetration were employed. This included drilling holes in the ears, pouring boiling oil or other corrosive chemicals in them and pelting them with blaring noises continually in an effort to unblock them. All were total failures and the victim remained Deaf as ever, sometimes more Deaf, and suffered agonising after effects. Pus poured from their ears, sometimes for the rest of their lives. Those subjected to loud noises ended up with permanent giddiness and unstable equilibrium.

Even the rich and powerful were not exempt from savage "cures". For example, the great Duke of Wellington after a lifetime of subjection to the roar of cannons became partially deaf. Whilst Prime Minister, he sought a remedy from an otologist who poured caustic soda into the ear making a partially Deaf PM into a profoundly Deaf PM. Wellington could not hear the names of a new cabinet read out in the House of Commons. After every name, he asked in a loud voice Who? and the cabinet became known to history as the "Who-who cabinet".

The most famous of all these unsavoury cure merchants was Jean-Marc Itard, a Frenchman, who entered the army and learned medicine while serving. On his

41

discharge, he assumed the name of Dr Itard and became interested in the study of lunacy. His thesis on treatment of asylum inmates won him recognition as a surgeon from the Faculty of Medicine. His connection with the Deaf resulted from his encounter with the Wild Boy of Aveyron who lived like an animal in a forest of that area and who was thought to be a Deaf mute. It awakened Itard's interest in Deaf people and deafness and led to his appointment as resident physician at St Jacques' School for the Deaf, Paris in 1800. He experimented with electricity on pupil's ears and used leeches on their necks. He also pierced eardrums but this led to discharge of foreign matter from the ears of one pupil who eventually died soon after the treatment.

News of a cure reached Itard's ears. One man regained his hearing after inserting a probe in his Eustachian tube, that is the passage between the middle ear and the back of the throat which serves to equalise air pressure on both sides of the eardrums. The probe was used to flush out lymphatic excrement and had been tried fairly widely before Itard's time and was found to be valueless. But Itard thought up improvements, believed to be made by pupils in the carpentry shop, that produced a metal headband to which a clamp was attached. It held a long silver probe that was thrust up the patient's nose. At every movement it penetrated the Eustachian tube, it caused intense pain. Irrigating fluid was then syringed up the probe and when the fluid reached the head the patient became dizzy and nauseated. Over 100 pupils underwent the treatment and none showed any improvement other than dire effects. Itard published several articles about it that won him acclaim as the world's leading authority of ear catheterising.

When this failed he resorted to herbal remedies, purgatives and caustic soda. He even tried to fracture the skull by striking the area behind the ears with a hammer. Most caused grievous injuries and life-long scarring. His series carried out for about 25 years were little better than systematic torture. Failure and parental complaints over the damage done to their children put an abrupt end to the demonic treatment. He declared regretfully that the dead ears were as good as dead bodies.

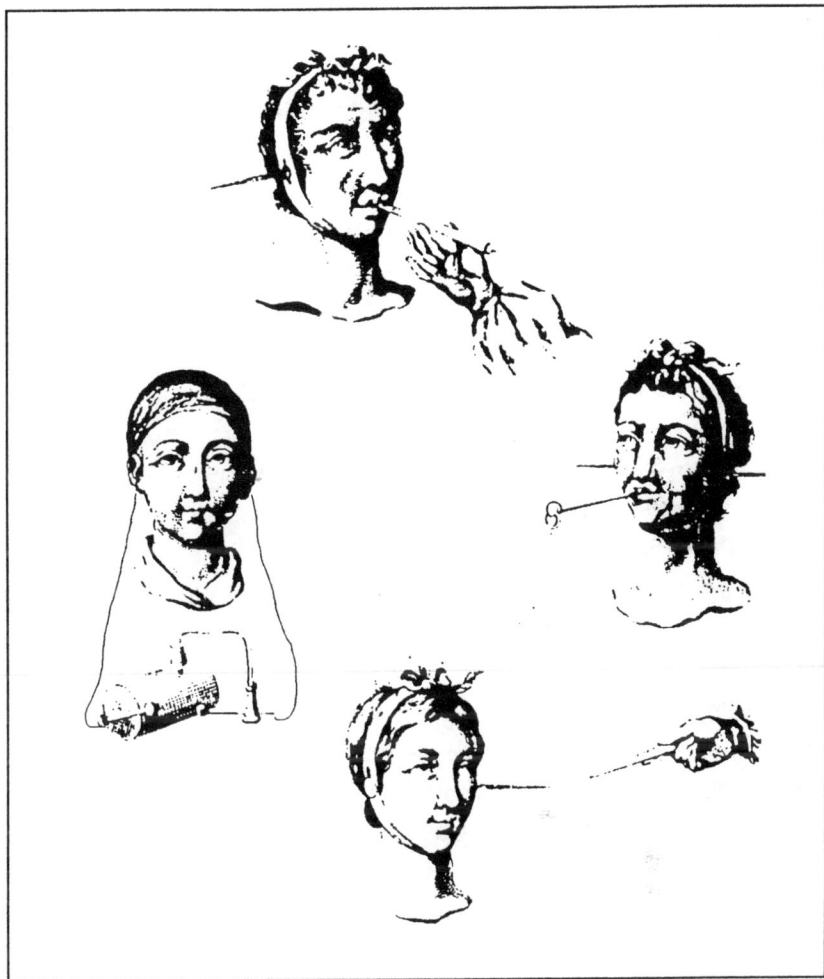

Some illustrations of early victims of Dr Itard's "cures": purgatives and corrosives injected into the eustachian tube; electro-shock terminals placed in the ear; cauterisations of the mastoid process and catheters inserted via the nose. These were extremely painful and of no benefit whatsoever in relieving deafness.

The Eugenic Road to Hell

Chapter Eight

People who set out to do good do so out of sympathy for those felt to be deprived, handicapped, disabled or sick. Basically this is the epitome. But there is a different kind of dogooder who puts self above those helped. Such a one seeks fame, finance or honour. Others go all out to crush opposition that threatens to thwart one's progress towards fulfilment. Such was Alexander Graham Bell whose paternalistic stance on behalf of the Deaf earned him more denunciation than praise from the people he set out to help. Bell's interest in the Deaf sprang from his father, Alexander Melville Bell, an elocutionist, who claimed to have invented Visible Speech. Actually it is a system of symbols already tried elsewhere. His son Alexander Graham maintained he used it successfully in teaching speech to the Deaf at a small school in London. When he established himself at Boston, USA, he opened a school to teach the system to teachers of the Deaf. He was just small fry, attracting only few interested bodies. He married a Deaf woman who was a former pupil of his, Mabel Hubbard, and used her as his model although her speech was anything but good. He succeeded in making her detest sign language to a degree of intensity although sign language was the preferred form of communication used by the majority of Deaf people.

By some stroke of luck, Bell heard of the experiment carried out by a German physicist which was transmitting sound by wire. In 1861, the man, Johann Phillip Reis, developed an instrument that successfully carried the human voice. He used a structure of a tiny beer barrel as the mouthpiece and sausage skin for the receiver. Bell's interest in the development was that he thought it would be a benefit to the Deaf, particularly to his wife. Whether or not Bell met Reis was never revealed but it appears that Bell destroyed every evidence of having contacted Reis. He made improvements that led to the patent of the telephone which was exhibited at the 1876 Philadelphia Exposition. The device, contrary to Bell's expectations, was of no value to the Deaf but an immense boom to the hearing. This elevated his financial standing.

44

11 years after Reis' death in poverty, a book by English writer, Silvana Thomson "Johann Phillip Reis - Inventor of the Telephone" appeared and caused quite a stir. The United States Government harassed Bell in 1900 about his knowledge of the German inventor's sausage-skin speaker from patent officers. But Bell had already sold his patent rights and was basking in wealth and fame.

His newly acquired status enabled him to pursue his passion as an Eugenicist. He had tried to popularise oralism among the Deaf and to get schools to adopt an oralist policy in teaching but his attempts, to a large measure, fell on stony ground. His enemy was sign language which the Deaf prefer and which, he was sure, was a barrier to learning and lipreading speech. He knew that it was impossible to stop signing in the Deaf community and schools, apart from the few oralist ones, that prefer the combined system which is speech and signing simultaneously. This was to ensure that pupils who have no aptitude for oralism to acquire imparted instruction easily. Bell knew that in this way pupils were apt to choose the easier method which is signing and neglect what is mouthed. When adult stage is reached most of them depended on sign language and its use led to the creation of Deaf communities. These were what Bell hated morbidly because the Deaf, he claimed, were prevented from integration into the normal populace that was Bell's aim through oral instruction. Nevertheless, there were signing Deaf people without speech who mastered hearing people's language, namely written English, and some of them were exceptional. This contradicted Bell's claim that the oral method was the best way to teach the language. He knew of these people but he always watered them down. His opponents who rebuffed his claims were such formidable characters such as Edward Miner Gallaudet, the head of Gallaudet College, the world's only liberal arts college for the Deaf at the time, and Dr Harvey Peet, another head. Deaf writers also attacked him.

Facing a lost cause, Bell sought refuge in Eugenics and in it he thought there was a way to to wipe out deafness from the earth. He believed, like most Eugenicists, that disease, proberty and criminal tendencies were the result of inheritance and that all could be minimised by selective breeding which means pairing the right people in marriage. In a nutshell, Deaf people are not the right ones. With money in plenty, he acquired flocks of sheep and at great expense, he tried to breed them into superior animals. He also studied blue-eyed white cats who had hereditary deafness. He wrote a number of articles about breeding that won him commendations. In some of them he recommended sterilization of impure species. Bell campaigned widely and succeeded in getting 16 states to have sterilization laws in force. Whether or not sterilization was actually enforced was not known but some parents, fearing Deaf grandchildren, had their daughters treated. An attempt, started by Bell, to make intramarriage among the Deaf illegal, promoted a Bill which was introduced into the Connecticut legislation about 1892. This law threatened to influence other states but it was withdrawn after a moving speech by Dr Job Williams, headmaster of Hartford Deaf School. Bell was heavily criticised and denounced as inhuman. Evidence against his arguments showed that most Deaf couples have hearing children and the majority of "Deaf" genes carriers were found among the hearing and the balance between the hearing and the Deaf having congenital children was much higher in the case of the hearing. Furthermore, the main cause of deafness in non-congenital Deaf children was a disease like Scarlet Fever and Meningitis.

Bell's actions in the area of deafness and Deaf people were immense which could only come from a person of great energy and wide knowledge, even if it tends to be destructive rather than beneficial. He stands out in history as the man bent on making deafness insignificant, doing away with Deaf communities through cultural genocide. The one good thing resulting from his actions was to make the Deaf aware of their rights and the threat of paternalism which enables hearing people to govern their lives. Simply stated, it means negative attitudes coming in the form of doing things for rather than with Deaf people as well as handling responsibilities, decisions, discussions and opportunities without input for the participation of Deaf people and preventing them from demonstrating their capacities. Deaf people's resistance to this treatment and campaigning for their rights began when Bell's force was almost spent. A more evil character in the person of Adolf Hitler took up where Bell left off - sterilization.

Barely 6 months after becoming chancellor and before he had obtained total dictorial powers, Adolf Hitler signed a law on 14th July, 1933, supporting his quest for racial purity under the titled "Law for Preventing Congenitally Diseased Descendants". It meant compulsory sterilization of every individual who were Deaf, blind, mentally handicapped or categorically disabled. Pregnant women so affected were forcefully aborted even if they had previously given birth to perfectly healthy children.

It was surprising that the law was met with so little resistance. School teachers may not have realised the import of new medical reports they had to fill out for Deaf pupils during the Autumn of 1933. But the intent could not have remained hidden from them for so long. Soon whole classes of adolescents and even children as young as 9 years old were taken by the school authorities to clinics to be doctored. It may have been that teachers knew that Deaf pupils could not remain at school unless they have undergone the treatment in which case, they put education before the sanctity of the pupil's bodies. Or it may have been that teachers, along with parents, knew that the law was difficult to avoid. But there were cases of institutional directors and teachers of the Deaf, who not only supported and enforced the laws against their charges, but often proposed even more inhuman steps to the authorities. Once a Deaf adult became known to a neighbourhood Nazi Party, the person was sent an order to appear at a clinic within 2 weeks or face serious consequences.

The leader of Germany's biggest organisation of Deaf people was made the tool of the Nazis and, although Deaf himself, was given an uniform to signify himself as a party agent armed with authority. He formed a crusade against the Jews which appeared in the organisation's publications and in it he eulogised the sterilization policy as doing an honour for the fatherland. He boasted about himself as being one of the first to volunteer and he said he felt elated and purified after the simple and painless operation. Those who hesitated or objected were swiftly reported to the authorities. A later edict "Mercy Killing" was the penalty for those who resisted. The church, perhaps through being powerless, remained impassive. In 1936, a

Lutheran pastor, assigned to minister to a Deaf congregation, delivered a sermon telling the flock that deafness is a pitiable condition from which future generations should be spared. In it he calls on them to accede to the law and offer up a "grateful sacrifice" for the good of Germany and mankind.

In addition, castration was fairly widespread. The choice between castration and sterilization for a male victim depended largely upon the caprice of the hereditary health judges who held court at the clinics.

About 350,000 Deaf and other physically and mentally handicapped people underwent the forced treatment and mercy killings. Among the Deaf, 16,857 people were involved. Alexander Graham Bell may have been horrified had he lived long enough to become aware of these chilling barbarities but it was an outcome of the very philosophy he advocated.

Deaf Jews were in the front line for extermination since they represented 2 disabilities. They carried genetic strains of being Non-Aryan and being Deaf. Some felt threatened and managed to escape abroad. A director of the Israelite School for the Deaf in Berlin, Dr Felix Reich, planned to escape with a number of children. He applied to the USA Embassy for entry visas but was refused as there was a restriction against Deaf immigrants to the United States but he managed to gain permission for 11 children to enter Britain. In July 1939, he reached Holland with them and finally made London where the children were accommodated and educated in English at the Jewish School for the Deaf at Balham, South London. Half the number later emigrated to USA to join relatives who sponsored them. All of them were denied the joy of having children.

With the hindsight of history, it is obvious that this perverted practice was covered by the perverted language of Euphemism:

"patients who are considered incurable in evaluation of their condition can be granted a mercy killing" said Hitler in October 1939, preparing the way for the legalised massacres of the 40's.

Left behind at the Berlin school were 146 children. In 1942, they were seized and transported in vehicles, bearing the euphemistic lettering "Humanitarian Ambulances Company" to the dreaded Auschwitz and Thierstentadt camps. The entire Deaf residents of the Berlin Home for Aged Deaf People were sent to these camps. Survivors were never traced so it was assumed that all perished. What remains to this day is a plaque on the wall of what was formerly that of the Berlin school's frontage. Written in German it records the seizure of the 146 Deaf Jewish children by fascist bandits.

Otto Weidt, an Aryan, ran a workshop in Rosenthalerstr. Berlin, in which he employed only deaf and blind Jews. Although infirm, this man belonged to the few Berliners who helped the Jews. He managed the workshop in such a way, ignoring the financial side, so that 125 persons employed could be occupied and get paid. Until 1943 he was able to save them but in the face of the "Final Solution" he felt his task to be hopeless. In January of that year all Jews employed by Weidt and their families were taken to the Gestapo Headquarters in Gross Hamburgerstr where a Viennese Sturmbandfuhrer accelerated a deportation order. But Weidt argued that his employees were working exemplarily for the Nazi war effort and this statement won a reprieve. He marched at the head of his band of deaf and blind workers, displaying the Yellow Star, through the streets of Berlin to his workshop. It was a march of silent demonstration against inhumanity. Barely a month passed when they were arrested again only to perish in the gas chambers of Auschwitz.

Ironically, after meting out harsh treatment to Deaf people, the Nazis encouraged able bodied young Deaf men to volunteer for military service. An unknown number actually did and served on the Western and Eastern fronts in 1944/45. Most were killed, believed to have been caused by being unable to hear commands. All records pertaining to these Deaf soldiers were destroyed when Germany capitulated. With no trace of any of them surviving, it was not possible to authenticate the story. However, there exists a record that refers to a totally Deaf soldier who served during the 1914-18 war, Wilhelm Kohler, a former pupil of the School for the Deaf at Altenburg, Saxe. He was awarded the Iron Cross for conspicuous bravery. Several other Deaf soldiers were captured and taken prisoner and interned at Yser, Belgium. After the war in 1945 when most educators who, however unwittingly or acquiescently, went along with the sterilization and mercy killing policies, were back in the classrooms again. When questioned about these acts they remained tightlipped and continued in their work as if nothing had happened. Deaf people were ashamed and afraid to say anything. Their parents were silent too. It was not until some 30 years afterwards that the full extent of Hitler's inhumanity to Deaf people became known. About 1,600 Deaf people were killed in the concentration camps. Some survivors owed their lives to hearing inmates who risked their own by answering for those unable to hear at the roll call.

Even before the Holocaust, the road to hell was marked by that combination of mercilessness, bureaucratic punctilio and perverted language that characterized the Hitler regime. Perverted or not, Hitler had a remarkable gift of spoken language which enabled him to impose his evil will on most of Europe. He was undoubtedly the greatest oralist of them all.

The Rise of Pious Paternalism

Chapter Nine

Before the turn of the 20th century a crop of missions emerged in most large cities in Britain. The initiative in founding such societies which occurred around mid-19th century that led to their establishment was generally taken by the Deaf themselves and in particular, by Deaf individuals possessing superior education or financial means. They were created through the need of social intercourse for Deaf people who would lead lonely lives cut off from their likes who use the same form of communication, namely, sign language. These missions were run by missioners, mostly hearing, who were all-powerful and all-knowing and whose competence in the use of the language was highly rated. Understanding between them and their charges were rarely in doubt thus creating a high respect for the missioners. They had the backing of the educated and literate Deaf who were at the beck and call most of the time. Their task, apart from layreading in church service, an important mission function, was to water down any form of ill feelings or criticism against the principles of the mission or the missioner. These places were drab and its participants led drab lives, usually going no further than home, work and mission. The unenviable task of the missioners was to find work for their charges, raise funds and scour the area for Deaf people, unaware of the existence of the mission, and to encourage them to take part in its life. To a large extent they were ill-paid and some were reduced to picking up clean tram tickets in order to claim a few pennies recompensation from the mission treasurer, usually an unpaid well to do individual who presided over the books with hawkish scrutiny.

The paternalistic attitude of the missioners created some resentment especially among those who possessed higher intelligence and who had little respect for religious matters. Some of them were banned from the missions for their stance or as an excuse for having been seen in a public house which was regarded in these days as sinful. Naturally, they severed all links with the mission and used public houses as meeting places for themselves and their fellow dissenters. They were the very people who, consciously or unconsciously, begot the feeling for the rights of the Deaf and their individual identity. Many years, however, were to pass before demonstrations by large numbers for these rights were manifested.

Missions in Glasgow and South London had their names changed to The Deaf and Dumb Temperance Association in an effort to show the public their abhorrence to drink and win appraise, an important inroad to funds. The South London missioner of this association, Ernest Abraham, claimed to have rescued a number of Deaf people from frequenting public houses, known to the anti-drink lobby as dens of sin. But there is little evidence to support this claim and much more to show that he was told to mind his own business, a rebuff which was one of the reasons for his emigration to Australia about 1900. The collapse of the London Association immediately followed his departure and it was some time before the Glasgow one went out of existence.

The missioners' task in finding work for the Deaf was made more difficult by the Workman's Compensation Act and the National Health and Employment Acts that compelled employers to compensate workers injured in the course of their employ. It was thought that Deaf workers were more liable to injury and this made employers reluctant to hire them. Furthermore, Insurance Companies often demanded higher premiums for Deaf workers. Some Deaf workers were forced by their employers to sign an agreement to refrain from making any claim for injuries. This practice was illegal but no Deaf person wishing to safeguard his employment would dare raise a question. In regard to Employment Exchanges, the Deaf had a real grievance. Like ordinary persons, they make their contribution towards insurance and employment. On the other hand, Labour Exchanges do not advance their claims for employment, in view of the fact that they are unable to support the case of the afflicted person as being suitable. As a result, the Deaf got little, if anything, for what they paid in. The interpreting need of the Deaf was another factor and this induced employers to think that they would have to call in an interpreter every time they wish to communicate with or pass instructions to the Deaf workers. A grant from the Ministry of Labour, however, enabled the London based Royal

Association in Aid to the Deaf and Dumb to employ workseekers to help the Deaf but most of them succeeded where wages were low and work menial.

The missioners' other task, fundraising, did not appeal to philanthropy as did the case of the blind or even in the founding of Schools for the Deaf. Factors such as the sparsity of the Deaf as a population group and community attitudes to their disability may have been adduced for comparative neglect by philanthropic sources. They can only appeal effectively to the charitably minded through interpreters. The basic incentives to the dispensation of charity towards Deaf adults were largely absent. Unless the donor of charity was prepared to master the manual language as used by the Deaf, he would be unable to make contact with them and obtain the warm glow of doing good which he received from the gratitude of the poor, lame and blind. However, Sir Arthur Fairburn, himself Deaf, and others helping him raised funds for the erection of the Southampton mission. The Rochdale mission gained independent funding through the providence of Sir James E Jones, whose interest in the Deaf was due to the fact that his son, Ellis Llwyn Jones, had been born Deaf.

THE ASSOCIATION OF MISSIONARIES *versus* THE BRITISH DEAF AND DUMB
ASSOCIATION

This cartoon which appears in The British Deaf Mute about 1895 depicts a "cock
of the walk" attitude among missioners. Their bombastic and paternalistic mien
enabled them to dominate the Deaf scene from the middle of the 19th century to
mid-20th. Deaf intellectuals at the time flocked to the newly formed British Deaf
and Dumb Association in hope to promote an apologist movement to cut the power
of the Association of Missioners but most of the salvoes fired fell on stony ground
as the majority of the Deaf community relied heavily upon the missioners for
various forms of assistance

The Suppression of Deaf Ability

Chapter Ten

Acquiring deafness beyond childhood in some cases creates character changes and behaviour attitudes. A striking example occurring before the turn of the 20th century concerned one William Gunn, who was a pupil of the Northern Counties Institution for the Deaf and Dumb, Newcastle-upon-Tyne, between 1896 and 1898. Prior to admittance to this school he worked as a pit boy. At the age believed to be 13, he was allowed to work at the coal face as he had the build of a man and exceptional strength for a boy. An explosion occurred while he worked and rendered him totally Deaf. Deaf men in those days were not allowed to work in pits excepts on the surface as screeners and in accordance with the education mandates of these days which compelled Deaf children to be educated up to the age of 16, Gunn was sent to this school. He was found to be difficult to instruct, although he had normal speech and near-average aptitude in language, and became an irritation to the teaching staff. He was said to have picked up a male teacher by the collar of the coat and hurled him across the classroom. He was expelled before the leaving age for being violent and obstructive. According to hearsay he was a model of good behaviour at home and work before going Deaf. The transformation stunned his contemporaries.

Gunn, on leaving school, had no difficulty in obtaining work as a labourer for a number of quayside firms at Newcastle. Employers found him a great asset as he was able to do 2 or 3 men's work for the same or lower pay of one. He was then very big in stature and tall. A regular feature in his life was getting drunk and disorderly which needed the involvement of the police. When one was sent to arrest him at a quayside public house, he managed to hurl the cop into the River Tyne. It became customary for a posse of 3 or 4 policemen to appear when Gunn was up to some mayhem. He was usually kept in a cell overnight and discharged when he regained his sobriety. Hurling him to court was found to be useless since magistrates let him off because of his deafness and inability to answer questions even through a sign language interpreter. A blow with a heavy instrument on the back of his head ended his life. His body was found slumped on Bottlebank, Gateshead, in the small hours one day. The assailant was never found. It was said that the police hailed his death as a deliverance.

There is a significant difference in the frame of mind of the prelingually and postlingually Deaf. Those who were Deaf before acquiring language and speech got used to normal people's attitudes towards them and most got through life in a self-created awareness. They show fury only when openly insulted or mocked for using an alien and visual language. The ones who lost their hearing after several or many years of its use underwent a marked change that became stigmatic which consciously or otherwise tends to lead to different behavioral attitudes. Their contemporaries either desert them or become lukewarm. The obvious cause is the communication problem. An individual conveyed to another era like Ancient Rome would encounter great difficulties in getting adapted to the life of that time. This is an example in a rather exaggerated form of the deafened fate. To lose one's hearing in an atmosphere where speech is a dominant factor is beyond doubt, traumatic.

In stark contrast to the misfortune of William Gunn was the case of Arthur J Wilson, born in London in 1858. Scarlet Fever at the age of 12 rendered him totally Deaf but he was amply educated and had adequate command of the language so there was no need for him to go to a School for the Deaf. Instead he indulged in reading and efforts to upgrade his writing till he reached the age of 15 when he entered employment as a wood engraver. By hard graft and self-teaching in his pare time, he reached a high standard of literacy that enabled him to throw up his trade and embark precariously on journalism. He wrote for several local papers and for the Deaf and Dumb Magazine edited by Rev Samuel Smith which earned him little or no recompense. Cycling at that time, about 1880, took a new trend and it became popular. Wilson was working as a bicycle maker and he engaged himself in cycle racing. He went over to Ireland to race against the Irish champion, R J Macredy. They used tricycles and sat betwixt 2 large wheels with a half-size front wheel for steering. He won the race and the 2 became close friends. Macredy and his brother edited and published The Irish Cyclist but they split up and installed Wilson as its editor. This was his first major assignment which was to herald his authority in the cycle trade. He wrote extensively in it under the pen-name of "Faed" which is Deaf spelt backwards.

1889 saw the invention of the pneumatic tyre and this gave Wilson immediate impetus. He was given a management position to manufacture the tyre and circulate its distinct advantage that gives speed and buoyancy to any wheeled vehicle. Very little impact was made so he moved back to London and started on his own as advertising contractor with the Dunlop Group of Companies as the nucleus. He employed a typist, girl clerk and errand boy. He soon became successful and moved to larger premises before finally establishing the firm of A J Wilson & Co Ltd in Clerkenwell Road. Staff numbered over 200 and all were expected to be able to communicate by the manual alphabet as Mr Wilson was a hopeless lipreader although his voice was almost normal with very little impediment. Dunlop's world-wide reputation was largely due to Wilson's labours and his journalistic talent. He became a widely recognised force and was honoured with the presidencies of the famed Great North Road Cycling Club and of the Road Records Association, the latter of which he founded. He was said to have initiated the Prince and Princess of Wales (later King George V and Queen Mary) in cycling and was instrumental in getting the King to become the patron of the Cyclist Touring Club.

He founded and financed the Cycle and Motor Trades Benevolent Fund, to alleviate distress among employees of the industry who have fallen on hard times, such as losing their jobs to younger and more energetic people or through sickness or slump. In these days, the workhouse was where the destitute were destined for and the thought of it greatly disturbed Wilson. He ran the organisation as the secretary on a voluntary basis with Mr W R Morris, later Lord Nuffield, as the chairman. Later the fund enabled the Home for the Orphan Children of Workers of the Allied Trades to be opened at Sydenhyam, South London. There, the orphans were cared for, educated and given a good start in life. Wilson's greatest philanthropic effort was the founding of the Hospital Motor Squadron during the 1914-8 war and afterwards. He was its commandant and it was his job to organise transport for 500,000 wounded service men from London hospitals for health drives, taking them to the river, golf and other clubs and theatres. He once filled the Albert Hall with 8,000 wounded men for an afternoon's concert. Another establishment that owes its existence to him was the National Hostels for Deafened Soldiers and Sailors. They were given rehabilitation courses to enable them to enter trades suitable for Deaf workers. The organisation later became a Government concern. During the war, he was up and going. With an ambulance provided for and maintained out of his own pocket, he was out at all hours during air raids, picking up the maimed and injured by bombs or falling buildings and conveying them to hospital.

He was the first Deaf person to drive a motor car and boat. He invented car mirrors which were soon to become compulsory accessories of the motor car. His interest in almost all forms of sport led him to donate prizes which are still in existence and bearing his name. His great friend and collaborator, Macredy, said that Wilson's great characteristic was versatility and that he appeared to be able to turn his hand on anything and do it remarkably well. His lack of this important sense of hearing, Macredy added, seemed to have developed an astonishingly active and acute mind which apparently enabled him to do the right thing intuitively.

One would surely have thought that with such a record as his, in spite of a terrible handicap such as being unable to hear at all, he would have received some official recognition in some titular form of the services he had rendered to the nation and to his fellow-men. This was not to be. He was awarded the OBE which he rejected outright. The only reason for this action was that others were made peers and knights for much less. One cannot imagine that the Privy Council at the time were somewhat terrified to award such a title to a Deaf person, no matter what the person had contributed. In spite of this thought there existed at the time a Sir Arthur Fairburn who was totally Deaf and an user of sign language but his title was hereditary. However, he won respect in higher and lower societies for his impeccable behaviour and generosity in giving benefices to innumerable causes. Wilson befriended him and together they made the public aware, although not very widely, of the altruism Deaf people are capable of.

Another Deaf person who was bypassed for an award, even for one of a lower grade, was A R Thomson, RA. This man was disowned by his father, a civil servant of high rank, because he preferred to be an artist instead of a farmer which his father wanted him to be. He struggled in grim poverty to establish himself as an artist, accepting commercial work for the price of a cheap meal. He had the great fortune, however, in getting noticed by the great artists of the time, such as Augustus John, Sir William Orpen, Wilson Steer and Sir Alfred Munnings. Through their influence and the merit of his paintings, he was made an Associate of the Royal Academy. His winning picture "The Pilgrim Fathers embarking at Plymouth" in an open competition and other acclaimed paintings upgraded him to full RA status. He submitted two paintings "Runners in Action" and "Seated Boxer" in the art section of the London Olympics, 1948. The latter won the gold medal and the other one a prestigious award. Thomson was the official RAF artist during and after World War 2. His painting of the Commemorative Dinner in honour of the air force in which the Queen and Duke of Edinburgh figured along with many distinguished personnel established Thomson as one of the greatest specialists in the difficult art of composite groups. Other pictures of similar nature "The Debate on the Address in the House of Commons" executed in 1962 and later one of the House of Lords were the first ever pictures or photographs of the interiors of both Houses so Thomson was the first person in history to record such scenes. Having painted royalty many times, he acquired the title of Royal Painter (RP). The huge amount of paintings Thomson created during his lifetime of 84 years, some of which are famous and others which are owned by the Queen failed to get the Deaf artist, who had no intelligible speech, recognised nationally. Once again, deafness is a major drawback not only in getting works of exceptional nature noticed by those in position to advise on awards but in various directions that refer to promotion and production. Apparently Deaf people's behavioral attitudes, though not strange or criminal, stand out as an impression that they are unacceptable on social basis in normal society.

The awarding of honours have been widely criticised ever since the first gong was struck. Some were honoured for what many never knew and worthy others, like Wilson and Thomson, ignored. Getting knighted for what was later regarded as a disservice was widely felt among the Deaf community. It goes back to the time when Sir James E Jones, a Lancashire cotton merchant, who had a born Deaf son, Ellis Llwyd Jones, gave £16,000 in 1919 to open a department in Manchester University to train specialist teachers to become proficient in sign language, thereby enabling them to give instruction to children in the language they understand. The donor used this means to communicate with his son and his Deaf friends so it was of little wonder that he made this generous gesture.

Teachers of the Deaf up to then were paid lower rates than ordinary school teachers but after training at Manchester they were able to expect better pay. One Irene Goldsack, a reputable teacher, became Reader in Charge of the department and in 1934 she transformed it into an Audiology Clinic to conform to her recently acquired belief that the Deaf must be taught to speak, lipread and use residual hearing. Sign language was outlawed and all new recruits were told that is bad for Deaf children and hinders them from attaining language competence. Eventually she was losing her hearing and in 1944 Alexander Ewing replaced her but together they carried on with the work and got married. Ewing was even more dedicated to the philosophy and assailed sign language like a preacher threatening hell-fire for those who err. However, he worked hard and up to 1955 his department had trained 680 and was knighted about the time he retired in 1964. This was the highest award conferred upon anyone working in the field of deafness and it immediately led to some controversy.

The Ewings treated deafness as a medical case and this led to the medical profession having decision making in the management, education and welfare of people they knew little or nothing about. One doctor, who had a Deaf patient brought to him with an interpreter, was astounded to find the patient unable to communicate with him. He thought deafness was overcame and every one so afflicted was able to speak and lipread every word of the language, thanks to Alexander Ewing whom he had often heard about. During the Ewing era, oral successes were not abounding in fact, the profoundly Deaf remained as they had always been, poor at lipreading and using unintelligible speech but what was worse, an increase of illiteracy and semi-literacy was evident, revealed through a number of surveys conducted among school leavers at the time. Periodicals for the Deaf experienced a dearth of contributions from budding Deaf writers. The ones of another age can be absolved for terming the era as the Dark Age of the Deaf World. Here the Privy Council were blind to the consequences created by suppression of sign language till surveys exposed the dire state of a negative education.

An example of deaf art in adversity from Nepal. Sent to a British friend from Sita Ram Maskey whose protest for better conditions for the Deaf Nepalese was misunderstood as opposition to the government, resulting in severe hardships in a long imprisonment.

Stigma Without Frontiers

Chapter Eleven

Ignorance and communication difficulties are the forerunners of peoples' adverse attitudes towards the Deaf, resulting in suppression of their inclination to congregate with their similarly afflicted likes and to engage in discussions that are not understood by the general public, particularly their relatives and teachers. Some evidence of persecution mania has been noted in remote villages of Third World countries, apart from the Urubu-Kaapor and Masasi tribes where the Deaf enjoy an enviable social environment with their hearing peers solely because sign language is used widely and encouraged.

Nepal, lying at the foot of the world's highest mountain range, is such a country where the lives of Deaf people are not all roses. When they talk in their particular language in the street, people are attracted and they shout to others, some coming from their homes, to congregate and shout in unison "lato", which in the Nepali language means fool. This vendetta drives the Deaf to seek remote or indoor sanctuaries for their social intercourse.

In this country, arranged marriages are a way of life. It is virtually unheard of for a Deaf person to marry another who is Deaf. According to Nepali beliefs, the reason a person is Deaf is because of some great sin in a former life, so to marry another Deaf person is bad karma and it is just not done. Consequently, Deaf people marry hearing people who in most cases, do not know sign language and many couples, even after years of marriage, still cannot communicate. The country treats women as second class citizens but Deaf women fare worse. They have hearing spouses who treat them as mere chattels, expecting them to do all the chores and submit to them sheepishly when carnal desire inflames them.

There is a thriving Deaf community and a School for the Deaf in the capital, Katmandu. In the teeming population, where customary beliefs wane, the Deaf get along much better than in remote areas. A number of them became good craftsmen setting up their own business. One such man defied tradition by eloping with his childhood sweetheart whom he met at the school and eventually married her. The families of the couple were furious and demonstrated strong opposition to the marriage by appealing to authorities to have the marriage stopped. On failing, they disowned the couple. The Deaf man earned his living by metal sculpture and his creations furnish Hindu temples and home shrines and the income went a long way to support his family in which case he had a certain leverage. The couple's children were all hearing, without any evidence of bad karma, and they acted as their parent's mouthpieces when needed.

Greece, despite its prominence in the cradle of civilisation and progress towards idealistic standards for its people, had been guilty of an apathetic attitude towards the Deaf in rural areas and on the many islands up to the present day. There is a great number in these places who were never educated. Most of them are tillers of the soil and menders of fishing nets, being fed and clothed by their families who never knew that there were schools for the Deaf in urban areas on the mainland and that education was paid by the state. Lack of information and low intelligence among the peasantry led these families to regard that the Deaf cannot be schooled. Communication between them and Deaf charges is by crude gestures. Money to these neglected people is useless as they do no know what to do with it. But it was noted in many instances that they were well cared for and deeply sympathised with by their families. In contrast, an elite clique of Deaf people with their own exclusive club exists in Athens. They were successful business people and professionals in the legal, financial and banking concerns. Most of them came from wealthy families who were able to afford private education or individual tutelages for them.

South Africa's apartheid policy, however, did not undermine the educational needs of the Deaf blacks. It is hard to find any of them even in remote and underpopulated areas, unable to respond to questions put to them. It is thanks to the various missions, mostly Catholic, which the Government helps in financial terms.

Lower than dirt is the term accorded to the Deaf in Thailand. To find employment is next to impossible so they have to live by their wits and skill of hand. A Swiss mission set up a workshop for them to do handicrafts and paint pictures to be sold as souvenirs to tourists. Deaf vendors set up stalls in the lucrative Sukhumvit Road where tourists throng to. They had to be there before dawn to get the best plots. But as the tourist boom in the country increased, other non-deaf vendors muscled in. They gesticulate to the Deaf ones to pack up and go elsewhere. If the Deaf refuse, the police are brought to the scene and threaten the Deaf with arrest if they refuse to budge. Up to the present day, Deaf vendors have diminished or gone to poor areas where sales suffer. Once there was a Deaf woman with a sewing machine in the street doing clothes mending and alterations but like the vendors, she was driven away by the police and she later became a prostitute like most other Deaf women and girls. As in the case of Nepal, most people of Thailand and neighbouring Malaysia regard deafness as a penalty for some sin committed in a former life and some, especially among the peasantry, believe that the worst crimes committed results in deafness and blindness for lesser sins. The police, in response to public fervour, have established a marked code that in all respects in unfair and without redress to Deaf people and even in law courts, the Deaf stand little chance of justice unless they have wealthy relatives with influence.

In most Third World countries, the Deaf were denied legal rights through being unable to utter the oath in courts. Many of these courts refuse to acknowledge the oath expressed in writing or sign language so those without speech or having unintelligible speech are legal outcasts. A significant example took place at a Cork court, Ireland, in 1829 when an army sergeant was charged with a brutal assault and rape of a Deaf girl, Mary Brien, who was uneducated and without speech. She was sent to a Dublin Institution for the Deaf and Dumb for evaluation and to have her story checked but the defendant was acquitted because the court ruled that the plaintiff could not utter the oath.

A different story emanates from the case of Donald Lang, an illiterate and mute Deaf black. He lives in Chicago in the highly civilised country of USA and despite ample facilities for the education of the Deaf, he was never educated or was probably found to be ineducable. In 1965 he was charged with the murder of a prostitute but was found unfit to plead through being unable to understand the charge. Consequently, he was sent to an institute to be educated for the purpose that he would eventually know what the charge is but after 7 years of compulsory class attendance, he was still found to be unfit to plead. All the court could do was to discharge him. But it was not long before he was again at the court on a murder charge of another prostitute. He was given a life sentence. In prison he was subjected to a gross act of humiliation. He was held down by 2 inmates, strong as he was, while a third one sodomised him. The incident almost destroyed his will to live.

Among Australia's aborigines, about 30,000 are estimated to be Deaf. This is almost   10% - doubtlessly a very high rate. These Deaf blacks are entitled to free schooling and subsistence during school age. Free vocational training follows. However, it was never an easy task to trace them or to persuade them to come to school. Those who are schooled are helped to conform to the average white Australian way of life. During the first few years, they usually succeed and turn out to be good workers but the lure of the bush is too strong in their blood. They are apt to drift back to their tribal ground in the Northern Territories and lead a primitive existence, living in shanty encampments. They receive generous unemployment benefit but most of the money goes on drink. The tribes make little or no effort to keep themselves clean, resulting in disease that contributes to the high incidental rate of deafness.

Criminals who mastermind plans tend to seek dupes so they would not get caught if things go wrong. A group of youths at Manxini, Swaziland, got to know a Deaf youth without speech and they befriended him in hope that he would be of some use to them. By using gestures they egged him on to enter a bottle shop, snatch a couple of spirit bottles and make a quick get-away. They promised to come to his rescue if he got caught. Naturally, the Deaf youth got caught by an assistant in the act but he resisted and tried to flee only to be confronted by some shoppers and, true to expectation, the group waiting outside bolted when they saw their plot flop. He gesticulated in an effort to make it known that he did the theft for someone else but the people in the shop thought he was able to speak and pretending to be Deaf and Dumb so they fiercely beat him and made him bleed in the head. Police, alerted by the shop assistant, arrived and asked questions but the youth failed to understand and replied thus by gestures. Eyewitnesses said the policeman slapped him several times ordering him to talk and to stop play acting as they were not in the mood for jokes.

The youth was led to the police station and remanded in custody to appear in court. He was given a short prison sentence although the court acknowledged that he was genuinely Deaf and unable to speak. No interpreter was brought to help and to explain that he was duped which might have given him a conditional discharge. The incident happened in February 1991, which brands Swaziland as a country that so blatantly lacks cohesion in the welfare of Deaf people. In this country, interpreters are scarce and there are no teachers able to communicate with them in sign language.

No place on earth surpasses the blatant discrimination against the disabled in a number of Latin American countries so strikingly different from their North American neighbours. Signing documents, casting votes and even making a will are banned to those who have the misfortune to be deprived of one sense or another or without hand or tongue. The discriminatory laws are found in civil codes and fundamentally in special laws. Disabled people in these countries have to struggle day by day against discrimination society imposes upon them. The founding fathers who lacked understanding about the real capacities of disabled people and these people, through fear, apathy or poor education, dare not stand up and demand their rights. Among them the Deaf fare worst as they have no voice.

Mexico's president Benito Jaurez passed a law in 1859 that hit at the Church's interference in Government affairs. It remains effective to this day but the church of San Hipolito adjoining the Institute of San Juda for the Poor Deaf and Dumb got into trouble over this law in 1977. The building stood over a subway in Mexico City and was under the charge of Father Angelo Alegro (translation in Merry Angel) who was Deaf and wore a hearing aid. The press accused him of trying to draw his 200-strong congregation by celebrating the mass in sign language. Reporters watching the service thought the priest was attacking the Government. The penalty for such an offence was confiscation, without compensation, of all church property. Fortunately, the reporters, not understanding sign language, failed to prove their point.

In Columbia, 100% of the educational agencies are administered by hearing persons, who in general terms, and with few exceptions, approach the Deaf community either with cultural arrogance and paternalism based on downright ignorance. These circumstances are common in most developing nations where Deaf persons have been tied to negative attitudes. In Belize, discrimination against Deaf persons is strongly felt and their human rights violated. Legislation protecting the Deaf and other disabled people is lacking and they have no access to administrative or political jobs and their salaries are not competitive with those of normal people. Even driving a car is banned to the Deaf. Education of Deaf children is poor so when they become adults they are unable to remonstrate or demand their dues through being unskilled in use of the language of the people.

Resilience Without Frontiers

Chapter Twelve

The first sign of Deaf people's attempts to throw off the yoke of hearing people's influence and guardianship occurred in France in 1830. A movement was formed under the leadership of Ferdinand Berthier who had Alphonse Lenoir and Claudius Forestier as allies. The 3 were educated by Deaf teacher, Jean Massieu, and they became the literary powers in the movement. Another one, Roch Ambroise Auguste Bebian, the son of an aristocrat who fled to Mexico at the time of the Revolution, moved to Paris in 1807 and was given the role of teacher's aide at the St Jacques School, founded by Abbé de L'Epée. He undertook a serious study of linguistics and published a number of works on pedagogy that won him the position of Pedagogical Director at the school. The reflections undertaken by Bebian on the role of sign language in education of the Deaf had a strong influence on the up-and-coming Deaf generation. However, a growing faction of hearing teachers was formed and they attacked the Bebian policy which did not support the oralistic approach. Their actions which comprised of insulting attacks on a number of practices infuriated Bebian and he, by nature, an impetuous man, struck another teacher, Louis Paulmier, in the presence of Abbe Sicard who was in charge of the school and who had elevated Bebian in his enviable position. He was immediately fired. He never again held any official position but his competence in the field was held in respect for many years even by his worst enemy. After Sicard's death, the directors of the school, all with religious backgrounds and with some understanding of education in general, were not scintillating masters in the adaption of pedagogical methods for special students. The school established an Advisory Board charged with reflecting and reorganising the curriculum but Bebian continued his combat outside the walls by publishing linguistic essays, pedagogical manuals, newspaper and magazine articles and anti-oralist pamphlets. The administrators of the school did nothing to stimulate the Advisory Board and little progress was made. Bebian's opponents grew older but not wiser. Classes were disorganised and teaching methods changed frequently. One teacher had not taught for 2 years; he gave his smartest student the responsibility of making other students practice their lessons. The student body said that the teacher treated them like dogs and they complained to the director and the administration but they were not believed.

Over the years, Bebian became the nemesis of the St Jacques school administration. He became weary of trying to secure a post in the school so in 1826 he opened a private school on the Boulevard Montparnasse. Shortly afterwards, furious on learning of the news, the administrators formally forbade anyone, teachers or students, to have contact with Bebian inside or outside the school. Although considered a nuisance to the school, however, paid lip-service to the value of his theories and manuals since there were none others to match. A delegation of 60 students approached the Minister of Interior complaining of the treatment of Bebian and a request for his replacement. This angered the administrators which led to the expulsion of 3 students, one of whom was Imbert, later to play an important role in the Deaf community. Ferdinand Berthier even had the nerve to send a petition to King Louis Philippe and this led to ugly scenes behind the walls of the school. But what surprised and humiliated the administrators was that the King invited Berthier and Lenoir to dinner and he even asked for news of Massieu and Clerc who had emigrated to USA to promote education of the Deaf. Actions, however, from the King were not promulgated but it was believed that the King's influence caused the hated rotation system, introduced in 1832, to end in 1836 and a couple of years later the Central Society for the Assistance and the Education of Deaf- Mutes was founded. Among its tenets was an acknowledgement that the Deaf person alone is able to correctly evaluate what Deaf students need and he alone is capable of proposing solutions to their problems.

In 1832, Bebian secured the post of director of the School for the Deaf at Rouen. But all his battles took their toll and his health deteriorated. In 1834, he departed for his birth place, Gaudalupe, Mexico, never to return. 5 years later, he died. His name implied the values that Deaf people hold dear - respect for the Deaf identity, the rejection of paternalistic attitudes towards Deaf people, and a profound understanding of the key role that sign language plays in their lives.

To counteract the Bebian method, in 1832 the administrators of the Paris School, that had about 130 students at the time, were influenced by the systems practised in Holland and Germany which gave priority to the teaching of speech and lipreading, a new method known as the rotation system was adopted. In theory, this oralist ideology which denied the importance, sometimes the very existence of sign language, sought to impose on Deaf people the means of expression and the ways of life evolved by and for hearing people. It was rejected as unjust by the students and most of the teaching staff. It gave vent to Berthier, Lenoir and Forestier, all members of the staff, to protest vehemently at the shameless enforcement which signified that Deaf teachers were not equipped to teach orally as speech and lipreading became mandatory. They were thus reduced to teacher aides on lower pay and Berthier, the most resilient, was given a class of failures, students whom the new system had failed miserably and from whom nothing was expected, but Berthier, talented as he was, turned them into good scholars.

The struggle for recognition of sign language went on when Ferdinand Berthier and his friends who shamelessly called themselves deaf-mutes, organised annual banquets in the French capital. The first one was in 1834 and it must have been inscribed as one of the milestones in Deaf history since it made the presence of the Deaf community known and the establishment of some kind of government for themselves. The banquets obviously brought together an elite - only some of the lucky ones who had been educated. Estimated numbers of deaf-mutes in France at the middle of the 19th century vary from 20,000 to 30,000 and in 1942 only about 300 of them had benefited from public education. However, 5 years later, the number increased to less than 1,500 although some 6,000 were in a position to be able to go to school.

Those in attendance were scholars, painters, teachers, civil servants and some elite foreigners among which were American artists, H H Moore and Douglas Tilder, Charlie Chaplin's actor friend, Granville Redmont and the Argentinian painter, J A Terry, came to later banquets. Berthier made some attempts to involve famous writers like Chateaubriand and Victor Hugo but he got no reply to his invitations sent to them. He, therefore, called on them and found both ill with the former almost paralysed and incapable of replying in writing to Berthier's questions. Hugo was confined to his bed and forbidden by his doctor to get up but he produced a brief piece of writings saying that he had no wish to treat the Deaf people as disinherited and went on with the following words:

"because Nature, in depriving you of one organ, has almost always doubled your intelligence. You, Monsieur, are a noble and dazzling proof of that you have the rare talent of being at the same time mute and eloquent!"

Invitations sent out to others, like journalists attached to the major newspapers at the time including The Times and civil servants from ministries that had charge of Deaf affairs were sent out and one such invitation by Berthier's hand in 1840 was as following:-

Recently there were some unkind remarks made about our fraternal association. It was said that nothing would be more disastrous for the deaf-mute than to limit himself to only the company of other deaf-mutes. To isolate deaf-mutes into separate nations, a special caste, would be to condemn them to a deplorable exclusion. Those who say such things have misunderstood what is in our hearts. Our spirits have never harboured such egoistic intentions of separatism. We have been rejected from banquets of hearing-speaking people. They wanted to suppress the language of deaf-mutes: that sublime universal language given us by Nature. And yet deaf-mutes have said to their speaking brothers "Come among us: join us in our work and in our play: learn our language as we learn yours: let us form one people, united by individual ties." My brothers, is that egoism? Is that isolation? Let our accusers with no conscience just dare again to raise their voices against us!

At one banquet the speaking audience who were present were given quite a show of it and it was said that banquets were the olympics of the deaf-mute people, olympics 4 times more frequent than those of Greece and a 100 times more exotic than appealing.

> *"It seems"* wrote one reporter, obviously dazzled, *"that 60 men deprived of hearing and speech should have constituted a painful and grievous sight: but no, not in the least. The human spirit so animates their faces, most of which are truly beautiful, it so shines forth from their lively eyes, it blazes its way rapidly to the tips of their fingers, that instead of pitying them, one is tempted to envy them. When, in the court room, in the pulpit, in the theatre and in society, we so often hear words without thoughts: it is rather agreeable to see, at least once a year, thoughts without words. It is no exaggeration to say that none of the orators, we most admire, could even remotely compete with Berthier, Forestier or Lenoir for the grace, dignity and the correctness of their gestures. In truth, seeing speeches that these three young men deliver is enough. I think, to make us wish we could unlearn speech."*

Banquet records describe the activities of its committee that led to the founding of associations destined to promote the interests and rights of the Deaf. The minutes of the banquets reveal the dreams, the plans and the struggles of Deaf people beginning to reach their full potential. The tradition of these banquets spread through France and then abroad.

Ferdinand Berthier died in 1886 and left a legacy in the form of the Napoleon Code which was mostly about Deaf Rights and the conservation of what comes naturally to Deaf people - sign language. The work was written in 1868 in response to The Civil Code of the French Empire. Many claim Berthier to be the first person in history to publish a Charter of Deaf Rights but a Judicial Recognition of Deaf People's Rights was published in 1863 in Russia and that was written by a Deaf graduate of the St Petersburg School for the Deaf, A. Sokolov.

Between 1870 and the end of the 19th century in France alone, there were 15 journals edited and written by Deaf individuals. Most, if not all of them, were educated in a sign language atmosphere before the change to the oralist scene created by the Milan Congress in 1880. The literary aspects of these journals were of high standard that seems to reflect upon the education system which the writers had gone through. One Henri Gaillard, who edited the Deaf-Mute Journal, wrote extensively in others and a lot of his writings were in defence of sign language and the promotion of Deaf Rights. He also made attempts to improve education, job opportunities and solidly Deaf Identity which he believed need not exclude Deaf people from the benefits of modern society.

Britain lagged behind the French in the publication field although the first one, The Edinburgh Messenger, was published in 1843 but it did not last. However, there was a series of magazines in succession from 1861 to 1903 which were edited mostly by hearing missioners. None of them had shown the fire of Gaillard in his quest for the betterment of Deaf people but some of the Deaf writers in the papers used elaborate language which would have graced a top people's journal. Most of them tried to outdo one another in literary standards. The first publication to show some fight and make attempts to redress the plight of Deaf people was issued by the National Union of the Deaf for a decade beginning in 1976. Lack of support caused its cessation.

America's Silent Worker came into inception in 1887 and it was known as "The Voices of Deaf Men and Women" and aimed to create a formation later to be known as The Deaf Community. Following 3 decades of growth, its writers became embroiled in a controversy that had long divided the Deaf and hearing communities. Indeed, administrators, teachers and others in America agreed that the journal had been an useful advocate of Deaf men and women. Its establishment was the New Jersey School for the Deaf and it was the school which dealt with the publication and financed it. But by mid 1920s, hearing officials within the school administration, desirous of transforming the school to oral methods of instruction, sought to restrain the impassioned writers who used the journal as a forum to defend the use of sign language and the combined method, now known as Total Communication, or teaching. Noted for their vigorous and wide range reporting, the once dynamic staff of Silent Worker was forced to retreat from this and other divisive issues. In the following years, relations between the Deaf staff and the school administration deteriorated. The superintendent, Alvin Pope, fired several Deaf teachers for insubordination. George Porter, the architect and editor of this national magazine, later resigned under pressure. Finally, in 1929, Pope terminated its publication, arguing that it interfered with the education of Deaf students. Not to be outdone, Deaf writers established The American Deaf Citizen and continued their defence of sign language and Deaf Rights. One paper may have been killed off but Deaf men and women shall not be silenced.

Prior to the advent of the 20th century, the Deaf in Russia started to widen their activities and organisations were created in Moscow, St Petersburg, Saratov and other cities. Main aims of these bodies were to liberate the Deaf from hearing people's subjection and their activities began to influence on upbringing, education and professional training. Since this period, their culture developed and gained prominence. Theatrics, art exhibitions, publication of writings and sports competitions flourished till the democratic process was interrupted by the Revolution in 1917. It was not till 1926 when the Deaf of Russia emerged as liberated but in a limited scope. Then a myth began to be circulated suggesting that all the later achievements of the Deaf became possible through the new regime which ignored past aspects in Deaf history. From 1917 to 1987, the notable successes of pupils and ex-pupils of the St Petersburg School for the Deaf were hushed up only because the school was founded by the Empress Maria Feodorovna, wife of Emperor Paul 1, of Russia in 1810. The same fate was shared by the second school to be opened in Moscow in 1860. The reason was that its founder, teacher and director was Ivan Darlovich Arnold, a Deaf painter born of noble family. At the time, Deaf people were recognised as judicially capable citizens and could work as office employees on equal basis as the non-deaf due to positive results of their education. The recognition of their capabilities and a series of judicial rights were established in the provision of Code of Laws of the Russian Empire Adopted in 1856 prior to S Sokolov's publication.

Education of the Deaf was grounded on the theoretical and practical legacy of outstanding Deaf teachers who left written works dealing with pedagogy. All this was destroyed when found to be out of touch with the new moral and political viewpoints of the Soviet system. Many schools, including the ones at St Petersburg and Moscow, owned large territories of land with large scale farm facilities, workshops and typographies. They were reduced, destroyed or confiscated. Virtually nothing remained of the rich libraries of the 2 main schools. Local leaders or commissars in towns and regions were assigned to deal with education and social affairs of the Deaf although some of them have never met a Deaf person or learned about their problems. The main principle of these bosses was their fidelity to the Soviet political and propagandistic course of the authorities. The rich heritage of the pre- revolution years was rejected and crushed into oblivion and a new history full of myths and misinterpretations was created.

Only now, when Russian political history has again turned full cycle, has the rich archive of their national record been laid open to scrutiny and the full immensity of their disinformation about Deaf Russia brought to life.

Deaf Prowess in Sport

Chapter Thirteen

There is some assumption that Deaf athletes, being able-bodied, should be able to compete with and emulate their hearing counterparts in most forms of sport. Unfortunately, this is not the case. Even though coaching has reached a high level of importance in today's sports, the Deaf sports enthusiast competing to achieve a high standard, generally fails to reach the desired goal and has to be content with a lower performance level. This is because almost all sports coaches rely upon lengthy talks on methodology to improve athletes' performances. The great misfortune is that few coaches are conversant with Deaf people who strive to excel and some of them have been known to have innate ability and obvious potential, but they were never helped and therefore failed to succeed. However, a fair number managed to become successful by sheer dedication and iron will even against opposing bodies which declared that sport is dangerous and unfitting for Deaf people. Misconceptions about the Deaf is due to them being regarded as physically disabled when in fact they are sensory disabled.

Before the 19th century, no records were found about sporting achievements of Deaf people apart from a travelling Deaf strongman who performed feats of strength in towns and cities. The first man to gain world-wide fame was the pugilist James (Deaf) Burke, born in 1809. He was orphaned and became a gutter urchin as a result. Although unable to read or write he was employed as a Thames waterman because of his apparent strength and willingness to work hard. An encounter in a public house owned by a veteran pugilist, Joe Parrish, led to him getting some lessons in the science of Prize Fighting. This sport was a brutal business, fought under rules that enabled men to inflict terrible injuries on each other. Burke, although a mere 12st 6lbs and no more than 5ft 82" in height, proved a matched for any man, bigger and heavier. When the British champion, Jim Ward, retired, the chief contender, the Irish champion Simon Bryne found himself, much to his annoyance, matched against the Deaf and dumb upstart. Fearful punishment was sustained in the early stages of the contest. Burke's arms became black and blue through stopping the Irishman's savage blows and his bare fists swelled to double the size from the punches he landed. Bryne took it all and was soon in a dreadful state. His head was a mass of bumps, his shoulders and chest bathed in his own blood. At the 99th round, Burke, who had been kept going on brandy, managed to summon up the last of his strength and caught his rival full on the face with a heavy right-hander. Bryne collapsed in a heap and had to be taken home unconscious. He was in a coma for 3 days before dying. The "Deaf Un" became the new champion and was soon on his way to America with Parrish. He was matched against Samuel O'Rouke in New Orleans for a purse of $1,000. The opponent who was a friend of the unfortunate Bryne, was a much bigger man but Burke found that he new little of ring craft and was able to punch him at will. O'Rouke was punched into helplessness when angry spectators cut the ropes and invaded the ring. Burke had to fight half a dozen assailants to save himself from being stabbed. Someone slipped a bowie knife into his hand which enabled him to hack his way out of the turmoil and flee on horseback without collecting the winnings. He stayed in New York for 6 years then returned to London. His last match was against Bold Bendigo. His fighting spirit seemed to have reached a low ebb and he lost in 10th round on a foul.

James (Deaf) Burke was undoubtedly one of the greatest fighters of the bare knuckle era. He might have been the world champion longer if not for Bryne's death which haunted him and people's fingers pointing to him. Because of his deafness, he thought they were calling him a murderer and this affected his fighting qualities. However, Burke was now known only for fighting. He rescued 4 children and a woman from a blazing house into which he dashed without regard to his personal safety. One of the children died in his arms. For a while he did some acting doing strongman feats but he succumbed to drink and women. He was found dead from Tuberculosis in a Waterloo area gutter on 8th January, 1945. he was only 36 and had not a penny to his account.

Deaf boxers who reached world class status was not confined to Burke alone. Italy produced Mario d'Agata, quoted in boxing journals as the Deaf mute boxer. He had trouble getting a licence because of his deafness. His manager spent much time and money fighting the Boxing Board for this permit and when it finally came, the Deaf boxer was almost a veteran. He won the European Bantamweight title in 1955 and was matched against the legendary Robert Cohen for the World Bantamweight Championship. It took place on 29th June in Rome. D'Agata was in trouble during the earlier rounds but he improved later and battered Cohen into submission in the 6th round. He became the first Deaf man in modern times to take a world title. The following year he lost to Alphonse Halimi on points in a disputed contest. The lighting apparatus above the ring took fire and burned d'Agata's shoulder. But the umpires rules out the incident and allowed the verdict to stand. Mario d'Agata retired and became a successful businessman and a generous benefactor towards the Deaf community by his native Florence.

Top class football is where the hopes of the ambitious Deaf footballer are apt to flounder. Major Frank Buckley, manager of Wolverhampton Wanderers, noted a talented player during a Durham junior league match and did not hesitate to ask him to join the prestigious First Division Club when told that the player was profoundly Deaf. This was in 1933 and the player, William Readman, a former pupil of the Northern Counties Institution for the Deaf and Dumb, Newcastle-upon-Tyne, was nursed to occupy the Wolves right wing but the following year he was given a free transfer and ended his playing career as an undistinguished minor league footballer. It was the Readman case that revealed coaching and communication difficulties and since then no Deaf player, however talented, managed to enter top class football. Managers, coaches and scouts know the pitfalls deafness creates and when told of some promising young player, they remain passive. This contrasts sadly with one who was highly rated during Arsenal's greatest years, the second half of the 1920s and the first half of 1930s. Clifford Bastin had a hearing impairment which did not seem to matter when he was chosen to play for England when only 17 and was christened as Cliff (Boy) Bastin. He occupied the left wing and was partnered with Alex James, reputed to be the greatest inside forward of the time. He and James used sign language, obviously of their own making, on the field and during training. Deaf spectators at Arsenal matches were enamoured in watching this silent exchange of messages but none ever suspected that Bastin was Deaf. The greatest goalscorer of all times, Dixie Dean, whose 60 tally in a year remains unbeaten, started to lose some of his hearing during his best years and most of it was gone in old age. Lester Piggott, the jockey, was Deaf and went to the Gorleston School for the Deaf in Norfolk but he appeared to get part of his hearing back during his teens. A speech impediment is a notable part of his being and this caused him to be a man of a few words. However, since winning 28 classics, some experts of the turf regarded him as the greatest jockey of all times.

Deaf racing cyclists seemed to have been helped along by their clubs and members. The register of cycling records give a glowing manifestation of an Essex club, Becontree Wheelers, and its team trio, Clarke, Eskhouse and Fell, who during the post war years broke national team records in numbers far exceeding anything in cycling club history. Nobby Clarke, the Deaf one, was an integral part of the team. His finest performance was winning the 5 mile invitation at the old Paddington track in 1944 in which the nation's top sprinters took part. He was honoured by his club with the Best All-Rounder Trophy. He collected gold medals at the World Games of the Deaf, Copenhagen in 1949 and Brussels, 1953. Another prominent cyclist was Malcolm Johnson of Rotherham, who was one of the nation's fastest short distance riders, clocking 52 minutes 28 seconds for the 25 miles course. Johnson, like Clarke, won golds at the Washington 1965 and Belgrade 1969 World Games. Clarke, along with another Deaf racing cyclist, Peter Stovold, joined the Fulham Wheelers in the early 1950s and they managed to recruit a number of Deaf riders but coaches and officials did very little to help or encourage them so all of them resigned. Stovold moved to Gravesend and raced in the Kent area competitions. After Clarke's early demise and Johnson's retirement from racing, Stan Gilbert emerged. He belonged to the Cambridge Town and County Cycling Club and was their champion for a number of years in the late 1960s. Although Deaf, the club made him their captain. His most impressive performance was covering 432 miles in a 24-hour road race. In Italy, the Champion of Champions, Fausto

Coppi, 5 times winner of Giro d'Italia (Tour of Italy), twice winner of Tour de France and the 1953 World Champion, and on friendly terms with the Pope, had 3 promising cyclists, G Cavani, C Carzaniga and S Servadei under protege. Helped by coaching and furnished with useful hints from their country's greatest rider, they were stunned into humiliation when Britain's Nobby Clarke crossed the finishing line more than 10 minutes ahead of silver medal winner, C Carzaniga, in the 100 kilometres road race during the 1953 Brussels World Games. However, with further help from Coppi, Cavani improved and with Clarke retired, won the next 4 100 kilometre events in 1957, 1961, 1965 and 1969. Coppi, however, died in 1960 but his valuable help lingered on.

Unlike boxing, wrestling was without any restrictions on deafness so the Deaf wrestler, with drive and brawn, had no problems in getting accepted by clubs and finding sponsors when potential is noted. Italy's Ignazio Fabra enjoyed help in coaching and finance from the National Sports Association, a Government branch, which eventually won him a world title in the Greco-Roman flyweight division in 1955. Harry Kendall was selected to represent England in the Rome Olympics, 1960. Later he turned professional in the heavyweight division. Other Deaf professionals were Mike Eagles and the better known Alan Kilby who won several championships and his many television appearances made his deafness known to viewers through his tendency to use gestures in the ring.

Other distinguished Deaf sportspeople who represented their countries in the Olympics were Gerhard Sperling, the walker of East Germany, R Windbrake, the woman runner of West Germany, the Russian hurdler, Viktor Skomarokhob, the swimmer, Jeff Float of USA and Australia's woman swimmer, C Fitzpatrick. The only one, and probably in history, to win a coveted gold medal was Jeff Float through being one of the winning US relay team during the 1988 Olympics. Although profoundly Deaf, none of them appeared to have had coaching problems and on the other hand, they were helped by their governing sports bodies, particularly the Russian who had direct Government assistance. But apart from Mario d'Agata, no profoundly Deaf sportsperson have reached world class status and this seems to support the theory that one must have all one's senses intact as well as being in perfect physical condition. It has been stressed that vision plays a prominent part in most sports and Deaf people are supposed to be more visual through having to rely heavily on their eyes but still managers and coaches do not accept this theory as concrete.

GREAT FOOTBALL MATCH. ORALISTS - v. MANUALISTS. Repulse of the Oralists. Manualists 5 GOALS. ORALISTS 1 GOAL

Antagonism between the oralists and users of sign language came to a height before the end of the last century. This cartoon which appeared in The British Deaf Mute displays a scene showing a manualist victory.

There is one, now deceased, who is held in high esteem in the USA. He is William Ellsworth (Dummy) Hoy, the first handicapped man to succeed as a professional baseball player in major leagues. His rise to stardom began in 1886 and for 15 years he was outstanding and much applauded when playing for such prestigious clubs as Cincinnati, Washington and Chicago White Sox. Being profoundly Deaf and without speech, he used signs to communicate with team mates and this enabled him to make history by inventing hand signs that are now widely used by umpires in all baseball games. The Deaf have been clamouring for his name to be voted into the Great Baseball Hall of Fame, established at Cooperstown, New York State, but for years he was outvoted or ignored. A prominent sports writer claims that Hoy's 2,054 hits in 1,798 games was better than quite a few "immortals" now enshrined at Cooperstown. Furthermore, the hand signs he is reputed to have invented were credited to an umpire named Bill Klem, 19 years after Hoy promoted them. As a result, this umpire was voted in the Hall of Fame and this show of irony exposed blatant discrimination which is thought to have been caused by the "Dummy" tag and being Deaf. It appears that a Deaf man enshrined might be a blemish in the roll of illustrious names. However, in 1951 the American Athletic Association of the Deaf established their own Hall of Fame and Hoy's name was the first to be enshrined therein. Hoy died in 1961, just 6 months short of his 100th birthday but the campaign to get him immortalised in the baseball history continues unabated till the goal is reached.

Deaf Resilience Today
Redirecting a Cruel History

Chapter Fourteen

The Deaf community built a world of their own and most of their efforts were helped along with the backing of their national associations and federations and the contributions from Deaf intellectuals who managed to emerge despite low educational facilities. Complacency, however, was never the community's reward, in fact, conflict was their daily menu. Being a linguistic minority invited hostility from so many who took a grim view of their language which was thought to be barrier to Deaf people's acquisition of the language of their nation and a creation of ghetto status for themselves.

Who are their adversaries, one may ask? Most of them are in the field of education - teachers, educators, advisers attached to education authorities and the medical profession who regard Deaf people as imperfect hearing people. For more than 2 centuries, education for the Deaf was a raging controversy and still is. On one side are the oralists who favour teaching the Deaf speech in order to acquire conventional language. The opposite side upholds sign language as they believe that it enables the Deaf the easiest access to knowledge and initiates them into logical thinking.

The oralists condemns sign language as a sure fire way to segregation and social isolation and believe that speech and ability to lipread would enable the Deaf to be integrated into society even though they know that no Deaf person ever succeeded in being accepted by society on a FULL social basis. Lipreading, once hailed as Deaf peoples' passport to the hearing world, is now regarded as overrated since the ability needed to lipread is too highly skilled. However, there are very few, who by fate, possess a freakish talent for being able to understand almost every word uttered in their presence. One such person was a totally Deaf American Deputy Sheriff, named McCoy. It was very difficult to convince anyone who encountered him that he was not able to hear a thing. Now acoustics have came to replace lipreading. The headmaster of a well known School for the Deaf in Britain claims that no Deaf person can be totally Deaf. All of them, regardless of degree of deafness, has residual hearing, he said. Acoustic paraphernalia is installed all over the school and the Deaf pupils are fitted with listening devices. Those who complain about the pain that assails their ears or being unable to comprehend the meaning of the sounds are quickly reprimanded and told to calm down and get along with using one's hearing. Pupils enter the school Deaf and leave deafer, thanks to the daily dose of ear bashing bombardment.

The advocates of the use of sign language in schools as an educational tool appear to have the strongest argument which implies that Deaf school leavers, who have gone through the oral system of education, end up with the reading age of an 8 year old, unintelligible speech and lipreading ability no better than that of an untrained hearing person. It is widely thought among the Deaf community that it is far, far better to be a content individual using sign language, even in conditions that have ghetto bearings, than exist as a sorry and obscure imitation of a hearing person.

The Deaf community have to fight to preserve their sign language and culture which is threatened by strong forces, some of which are backed by legislation. The Warnock Report (1978) requested that the handicapped be integrated into normal society, resulting in the closure of special schools for the Deaf and Deaf children being forced into normal schools thus missing out in classroom instruction. A notable contribution this mainstreaming created was an increase of illiteracy and no marked improvement communication interaction between the hearing and the Deaf. Other forces are educational advisers, like the peripatetic teacher telling hearing parents of Deaf children to persist in speaking to them and to treat sign language as an evil that would block their way to normalisation. These parents are promised the earth and when their children grow up to become unresponsive adults with poor speech and low education, they realise their mistake. These people were advised not to let their children get to know Deaf adults and when the children grew up, they became the very people whom they were told to detest. There are plenty of people about with an inborn and inveterate aversion of sign language and no means of hypothesis could convince them as to loosen, even slightly, their grip on their distorted belief. Others, not able to understand sign language, feel deprived when within eyeview of Deaf people signing and get driven to condemn such language as they believed it was talked in secret about themselves, sometimes resulting in fighting between the hearing and Deaf. Finally, Deaf people's self-image affected by the strong stigmatisation which society often renders to them and shows a tendency to discredit the sufferers by reacting as if they are also intellectually impaired rather than being merely Deaf. It seems difficult for some people to understand that it is only the hearing mechanism which is faulty - not the whole brain!

Some teachers, known to harbour such hatred for sign language, have been accused of running a vendetta against signing pupils. Some, caught using sign language, were deprived of cutlery and forced to eat their dinners with their bare hands to comply with their preference to use hands. Some Deaf persons incorporated into hearing values so deeply felt ashamed to be seen using signs. Oralist factions of Deaf people have existed for a century or so and they had an inbred antagonistic attitude towards Deaf users of sign language. In France at the turn of the century, a publication "Le Sourd Parlant" (The Speaking Deaf) was launched, probably to establish oralists as a group in opposition to the Deaf community, but it very quickly went out of circulation. The critics said that so very few oral-educated Deaf people could read so it turned out to be useless to the majority.

An old ploy readily available to families, some very wealthy, with a Deaf family member, regarded as a liability, was to get their charge certified as mentally defective. Any doctor finding the patient unable to respond to questions, had just to sign and the patient is confined to a mental institution for life and the family find themselves free from an embarrassment. Being without the means to communicate, such patients just can't remonstrate. A fairly large number of Deaf people were known to be confined to such institutions at the turn of the last century. Some were released when found to be perfectly sane but others who have been instituted for years just can't cope when outside so they had to be returned to the life they got used to.

Another towering menace is paternalism. Well meaning do-gooders, some with great influence, tend to take decisions on behalf of those they sympathise with. Educators, backed by Governments, provide programmes of education for Deaf children whom they know little about. Unknown to them, the profoundly Deaf are inclined to have a thought process that is not the same as the hearing. Hearing people use internal speech to do their thinking. The Deaf often tend to use pictorial thinking (Dimmock - Introspections on the Deaf Mind, 1986). The way Deaf people think justifies the need for sign language as a classroom instruction. It is pathetic for a class of people, whatever their hearts or pocketbooks or academic background, to involve themselves in decision-making in an area completely outside their ken.

Against overwhelming odds, the Deaf community continue to exist and grow in strength and their awareness campaigns have won public respect in large measures. Sign language is now understood as a highly expressive and intelligent means of communication thus qualifying the Deaf as a linguistic minority. After years of battering, they are likened to the McGregor clan, although persecuted cruelly, continued to flourish in their untrammelled path and sang defiance (Montgomery 1992).

In 1983, the Swedish Government officially recognised Swedish Sign Language as a native language of the country and their Queen took up sign language lessons and became fairly competent. This has set a crucial world precedent, an objective for the Deaf in order to achieve political recognition as a distinctive sociocultural group rather than a scattering of disabled individuals requiring State Charity. A distinctive trend is the establishment of sign language teaching centres where Deaf people with competent skills teach the hearing the language that was ironically denied to the rightful people, namely the Deaf, for so many years. A belief, now being evident, is that the hearing find it easier to learn sign langauge than the Deaf are finding in learning hearing people's language. Courses are booming and what if a large slice of the population can sign and Deaf people cease to strain their eyes in an effort to understand lip movement? Would it lead to a re-creation of Martha's Vineyard of a bygone era?

As the turn of the century approaches, Deaf communities can look forward to a tolerant society, no longer mocking their use of sign language and becoming more aware of their problems and cultural aims. The increasing use of sign language programmes on the television also contribute to the spread of awareness of and tolerance towards the Deaf. But something threatens this newly found complacency. One is the cochlear implant, now in experimental stage. It is part of a general movement to aid, control, modify and normalise unacceptable deviant behaviour (Montgomery, 1990). The message is clear; the threat ominous. Scientists are sparing no effort to perfect it. If perfection is reached, deafness might become defunct, sign language a dead language and Deaf communities fall to genocide. The Times once highlighted a headline "Deafness is Abolished" during the Ewing era when it was thought that every Deaf person can lipread everything that was being said. The media, ever ready to regard Deaf communities as a social shame, acclaimed to high heaven when the first cochlear implant was performed. It restored faith to the oralists and their backers and raised the hopes of parents of Deaf children. When Deaf people acquire hearing they might have to undergo the gruelling process to transform themselves to a hearing person, which is believed to be fraught with difficulties after having been Deaf for life. Such is the fate or blessing prescribed to the Deaf by scientists if they successful in their quest to conquer deafness. Many Deaf people who have been Deaf all their lives would, naturally, object to such a transformation but what if they are forced to have the implant just as Hitler forced sterilisation? Unlikely you may think, but you would be wrong. Already in USA, UK and Australia, children are being implanted without their consent, being railroaded into it by the same unholy alliance of parents, doctors and oralist teachers who have been attacking the Deaf community and their language all their life.

Conclusion

In reality, being Deaf is not traumatic. Most Deaf people who were so afflicted for the greater part of their lives manage to adapt themselves to the handicap and manage quite well. It is those who became deafened in later life that find the adaption difficult. The real tragedy lies in the consequences of deafness. Almost everything is geared up for the orientation of what the ears perceive. Society relying heavily on what is heard intentionally or unintentionally, creates barriers that confront the Deaf. Deaf activists all over the world spent time and energy to remove them or at least lessen the confrontation but they achieved little. The greatest is the medical model giving the doctor, the language pathologist, the language therapist and the audiologist an earthly right to say what the Deaf can do and what they cannot. Most decisions that govern the lives of the Deaf in the area of education, social standing and employment rests on this team, whether they are knowledgable about Deaf people or not. The result is that the education of the Deaf is in shambles; their access to employment is littered with obstacles; their place in society is such that they are at best, ignored or pitied.

In 1983, 2 Members of the British Parliament, Jack Ashley and Robert Wareing, in their Private Member's Bill tried to outlaw discrimination against the disabled but their Anti- Discrimination Bills failed to be passed, thus resulting in discrimination continuing to be legal. Any employer interviewing a Deaf job applicant would be legally justified in saying "We do not want Deaf people. Go away."

Some employers are not keen to use such blatant discrimination to turn away a Deaf workseeker have a ready answer in the form of the medical resolution which states that a Deaf person is a danger to himself. Insurance companies are known to use it to refuse to insure Deaf motorists or workpeople engaged in handling machinery. Some insurance firms find it an excuse for imposing a heavier fee along with ineligibility to compensation in certain cases of accident.

The Deaf of Sweden and USA, by campaigning and lobbying, have came within sight of forcing authorities not to rely on the medical focus relating to Deaf people. They preferred the promotion of socio-linguistic and anthropological framework instead. To get this implemented is an uphill struggle as a deep and detailed explanation in convincing aspects would be needed.

Dead ears are useless by doctors and their owners' behaviourial traits and social inclinations are absolutely irrelevant to medical science.

What the Deaf community can hope for is that posterity provides some dynamic person with the ferocity of Umai of Tinnevelly, the sagacity of Emmanuel Philbert and the wizardry of Dummy Hoy to bulldoze through artificial barriers worse than the Berlin Wall and correct absurd legislations and divergent decisions that since the birth of civilisation, have weighed Deaf people down to a position where humanitarian principles can be ignored with impunity.

Bibliography

Abraham E - The British Deaf Mute, 1896.

Abramov I A - History of the Deaf in Russia: Myths and Realities.

Adamson Rev W W - Council of the Church Missioners to the Deaf and Dumb,

Minute Book, July 1916.

Addison W H - Deaf Mutism, 1896.

Baird W - Report of the 1953 International Games of the Deaf at Brussels.

Bastin C - News Chronicle, Newspaper Library, North London, April 1933.

Berthier F - L'Abbe Siccard, 1873.

Braddock Rev G C - Notable Deaf Persons, 1975.

British Deaf News - 1955-1991.

British Deaf Times - 1938-1955.

Buchanan R - Silent Worker. Newspaper and the Building of a Deaf Community,

1887 - 1930.

Buckley Major F - "Wolves Topics", 1958.

Burke T - "Deaf Burke", ABC of Sport, 1973.

Calafelly P A - Historical Extracts, 1955.

Cartwright B - Silent News, 1990.

Conrad R - The Deaf School Child, 1979.

Dimmock A F - Instrospections on the Deaf Mind, 1986.

Dimmock A F - Nobby Clarke, British Deaf News, January 1991.

Dimmock A F - "Tommy", Scottish Workshop Publications, 1991.

Dimmock A F -"Sporting Heritage". SWP, 1991.

Fresquet R - La Gazette des Sourd-Muets, 1956.

Gaillard H - Le Journal des Sourd-Muets, 1904.

Hay J A - IYDP Address, 1981.

Hay J A - Scottish History Extracts, 1988.

Hodgson K - The Deaf and their Problems, 1953.

Holmes A M - Milan & Me, 1980.

Karacostas A - Education and the Birth of Deaf Movement in France.

Lane H - When the Mind Hears, 1984.

List G - A Suppressed Part in German General History.

Lovett J - CISS Handbook, 1975-1985.

Marroquin J L - Ponce de Leon, 1960.

Montgomery G - Beyond the Cochlear, 1990.

Montgomery G - Introduction to Deaf Liberation, 1976-1986. 1992 NUD.

Mottez B - The Deaf-Mute Banquets and the Birth of Deaf Movement in France.

Northern Counties School for the Deaf, Records.

Plann - Fray Pedro Ponce de Leon: Myth and Reality.

Quartararo A T - Henri Gaillard in late nineteenth century France.

Reuben-Alcais E - La Gazette des Sourd-Muets & Sportsman, 1953-1955.

Tidyman E - Dummy, 1973.

Thomson S - Johann Phillip Reis, circa 1885.

Truffaut B - Cahiers de l'Histoire des Sourds, 1989-1991.

Warshawsky L - Spotlight, 1970-1990.

Welsh General - Commander of British Army in India, Memoirs, Imperial War

Museum.

The Author

ARTHUR FREDERICK DIMMOCK emigrated to London as a refugee from unemployment just after the depression of the late 1920's. Despite being profoundly deaf he was well educated in the English language at a time before the ill judged prohibition of Sign Language made such an education impossible. He is now the foremost journalist in deaf society and a great example for the well educated deaf children in schools today. He has written on the psychology of deaf children in "Beyond Hobson's Choice", recorded the history of deaf peoples achievements in athletics and games in "Sporting Heritage" and his biography of "Tommy" Thomson, the distinguished deaf painter, is a remarkable story of the single minded triumph over adversity. Like Thomson, Mr. Dimmock learned how to conquer the Everests within before he ascended to the heights in his own career. His present book "Cruel Legacy" is the result of a working lifetime of experience corresponding with and visiting deaf people in every corner of the globe for his regular newspaper column "Girdle Round the Earth".

The photograph shows the author (on the right) at The 1990 BDA Centennial Conference at Brighton with godsons Murray Holmes and George Montgomery. Shortly after this conference, Mr Dimmock, an enthusiastic swimmer, accidentally swam into some chemical pollution in the English Channel but has now been completely detoxified.